PRISONER DOCTOR
An Account of the Experiences of a Royal Air Force
Medical Officer During the Japanese Occupation of
Indonesia, 1942 to 1945

PRISONER DOCTOR

*An Account of the Experiences of a Royal
Air Force Medical Officer During the
Japanese Occupation of Indonesia,
1942 to 1945*

Richard Philps
M.B.E., M.D., D.P.H., F.R.C. Path.

The Book Guild Ltd.
Sussex, England

[1]Mrs. E.L.F.M. Philps, Woodlands, Sydenham Wood, Lewdown, Okehampton, Devon EX20 4PP

[2]Hollinshead & Co., Bristol & West House, 4c Duke Street, Tavistock, Devon PL19 0BA

The Book Guild Ltd.
25 High Street,
Lewes, Sussex

First published 1996
© E.L.F.M. Philps
Set in Times
Typesetting by Acorn Bookwork, Salisbury, Wiltshire
Printed in Great Britain by Antony Rowe Ltd.
Chippenham, Wiltshire

A catalogue record for this book is available from the British Library

ISBN 1 85776 098 0

CONTENTS

ACKNOWLEDGEMENT

The men who survived Haruku and subsequent camps have reason to be extremely grateful to Leslie J Audus, Professor (now Professor Emeritus) of Botany at London University. Professor Audus was with us as a prisoner, having joined the Royal Air Force as a scientist and become a Radar (then called 'Radiolocation') Officer. During our first critical time at Haruku, with deaths from beriberi mounting and blindness from vitamin B deficiency on the increase, he, at first single-handed and later with a Dutch botanist, Dr (now Professor) J G ten Houten, devised a method of producing yeast, an abundant source of vitamin B. This was against almost impossible odds and with the most primitive equipment, but it was so successful that the onset of blindness was halted in those already affected, no new cases occurred, and other changes due to vitamin B deficiency began to improve – a remarkable feat of biological manipulation.

Professor Audus has recently described his methods to me in great detail and I have included them in Chapter 4. I have also included a reference to a Dutch book published in 1982 on the same subject (p. 101).

I take this opportunity of thanking Professor Audus for his brilliant work in this respect, for reading the manuscript and for translating passages from the book mentioned above.

*To those of us who died so
tragically and amid such squalor,
but among friends.*

FOREWORD

I have long felt that this account should be published as a tribute to the many young men who did not return and the few who still survive.

I am one of the lucky ones; my husband did come home and I feel enormous gratitude for 50 very happy years and the joy our family has brought me.

Emmie Philps

PREFACE

I volunteered for the Royal Air Force Medical Service after qualifying as a doctor in 1939, and was posted to RAF Mount Batten, Plymouth. There I met Emmie, who lived on the Hoe and was working as an interpreter and teaching the Polish Navy to speak English. We married in April 1941, and I was posted to RAF Dyce at Aberdeen. A few months later I was posted overseas. My account starts at this point.

There are two references to Christ's Hospital. I was a Blue-coat Boy (a pupil at Christ's Hospital, Horsham, Sussex), and feel that the groundwork of discipline instilled there had a great influence on my survival in the extraordinary conditions I was to encounter.

Richard Philps

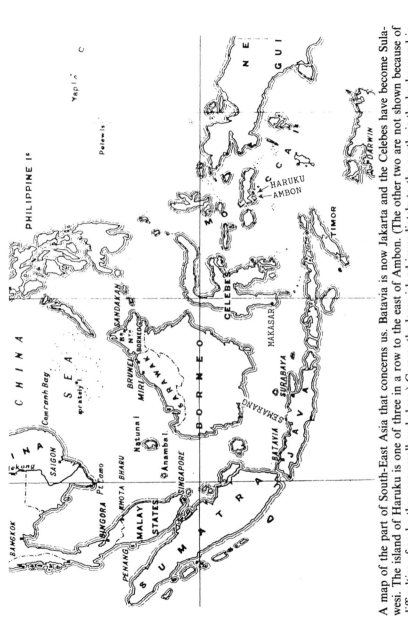

A map of the part of South-East Asia that concerns us. Batavia is now Jakarta and the Celebes have become Sulawesi. The island of Haruku is one of three in a row to the east of Ambon. (The other two are not shown because of difficulties of scale; they are small and close.) Ceram, the large island immediately to the north, is the background in the paintings in the plate section.
Use of map by courtesy of The Imperial War Museum, London.

1

INTO THE BAG

On 5 November 1941, on Aberdeen station in the evening, less than a year after we first met, I parted company from Emmie to embark on my overseas posting. I shall through all my days remember the feeling of hopeless desolation, the total inadequacy of words, the nearly certain knowledge that we would never see each other again, the bitterness beyond tears. Such partings were commonplace during the war, but for each pair it was a unique and dreadful moment. I suppose not to have experienced it is not to have lived – it is the reverse side of the total involvement that is love. We had seized our happiness and for that we had no regrets. Death was far too close at that time and every moment too precious for there to be any delay, and now, it seemed, it must all come to an end.

I went to Wilmslow to join a ship at Liverpool, bound for I knew not where, but we had drawn tropical kit. Emmie went to Mother's for a short time before she took up a wartime job in a boys' prep school in Dorset. (All the Poles had by now learned English, so she was no longer needed as an interpreter.)

Our voyage, in convoy, was not particularly eventful and my mind, in any case, was dominated by the misery of our recent parting. One had to learn to write letters which would be opened by the censor, therefore it was impossible to be uninhibited; the result at first was stilted and horrible. We spent our time playing deck games, drinking rather too much pink gin and, round the Cape, being seasick or nearly so.

We stopped for a few days at Durban and were fêted by the community, who made a prodigious effort – purely from the

1

goodness of their hearts – to give us a good time. Any unattached bachelor could, if so inclined, have had a rare time, so warm-hearted and lavish was the hospitality. I was not in the mood; I was far too close to my parting from Emmie, but I did manage to send her a tin of pineapple and – luxury then unknown in England – a pair of silk stockings (wrong size). We had become so used to war that to have all the lights on and no blackout precautions in the evenings seemed almost immoral. We were grateful to the people of Durban: the whole thing was so generous – and appeared so spontaneous, though no doubt a great deal of organisation must have gone into it.

We set out across the Indian Ocean, and when we passed the exquisite Maldive Islands our destination was clear. We were going to Singapore. The only event that stays in my mind, apart from my first experience of prickly heat, is the fact that we caught fire. We were passing the volcano Anak Krakataoa in the Sunda Strait in Indonesia. It was night-time and we were having film show. By some mistake, inflammable film had been included with the more usual – indeed, almost universal – non-inflammable sort and, rather spectacularly, the picture on the screen suddenly went up in flames. It took a moment to realise what was happening and when we looked back, the projection booth was on fire. The fire spread to part of the cinema before we managed to get it under control and for a moment, the cinema being on deck, we were in full view of any submarine for miles around. We were very conscious of the recent disastrous loss of our two big ships, *Prince of Wales* and *Repulse*, and that now the Japanese had rather too much freedom of the seas. We were lucky: there was nobody about. We arrived in Singapore in January 1942.

Singapore was a strange place at that time: it had not successfully made the change from peace to war. Used to a quiet, gentle, sociable life, the British inhabitants had not yet come to terms with the fact that the Japanese were dangerously close. Parties went on, petrol seemed freely available and, most remarkable of all, we were expected to go to bed in the afternoons. The amount of work required from a white man in the tropics was not great and war had done nothing to change

2

that. We had pathetically few aircraft, no big ships, and the Japanese bore down upon us through Malaya as fast as their armour – and their bicycles – could move. Soon, gunfire could be heard, at first distantly, and daily closer, and air raids on our airfields became daily events. We found that those of us recently out of Britain were so used to raids that we took them in our stride, but those to whom they were a new experience were very shaken by them. In fact, my ambulance driver, an Australian, had to be sent home with a nervous breakdown after he and I had nearly received a direct hit on a routine run one morning.

I did precisely nothing medical in Singapore, except standby duty for my more senior colleagues, which meant my sleeping in the administrative offices every second night. What they did with the time they were so released, I shall never know. If ever a journey appeared unnecessary, it was mine.

The Japanese were not expected to advance across the marshland to the north of Singapore Island, regarded as impenetrable, but did so without difficulty and took the island defences by surprise. Ships were available (I think, two) to evacuate the civilian population and such troops as were no longer needed, and it was my unenviable task to select those of the walking sick who would be better out of the way. I regret to have to say that I was greatly troubled by people malingering in the hope of getting out.

One sergeant I particularly remember because he set out to convince me that he had had a nervous breakdown – he simply came into my room, sat himself down on the floor and stayed there mouthing obscenities. Rather interestingly, he had just learned the word *lagi*, which is the Malay for 'more' (a word he would be using a lot in the Oliver Twist existence we were going to experience later). The word obviously appealed to him, because, whereas with some troops every second word was 'bloody', he had substituted *lagi*. He had nothing to say anyway, but it made a change. I finally had to have him removed by the Military Police.

There was also, I regret, a colleague, a young doctor, who managed to swing the lead to such effect that he persuaded

3

one of the medical staff to invalid him home because he had short sight and had broken his glasses. The way things were going, it seemed inevitable that doctors would be valuable, making this sort of conduct even more despicable, though probably we were better without him. If he reads this account, he may well reflect.

Another incident, pathetic in its way, had its droll side. Two medical officers, used to the soft life of Singapore in peacetime, decided that they needed to go home urgently, so they arranged to certify each other as medically unfit for further service in the tropics. I do not know what diagnosis they favoured, but the time came for certification and the senior of the two certified the slightly less senior as unfit. Then a dreadful difficulty arose: the one certified as unfit was immediately and automatically deemed unsuitable for further duty and was therefore not in a position to certify his senior colleague. This was deadlock. There were other medical officers about, including myself, but the uncertified one could not really order anyone to certify him as unfit, so the junior of the two left and the senior one remained. This was, in fact, rather sad, because he *was* unfit, both temperamentally and from the point of view of skill, to do anything useful in the medical field and would have been better out of the way.

The two ships left and we stayed behind to organise ourselves in the defence of Singapore. The British civilian population had all come to the dock in their cars, bringing what personal belongings they could and they abandoned them on the dockside. Literally thousands of cars were parked there and in the nearby streets, ownerless, after the ships had left. Anybody needing a car, even for a short journey, took the nearest one, drove it until the tank was empty, abandoned it and took another one. I drove several in those last desperate days.

I was suddenly ordered to go to Java by any ship I could find to set up the medical services for a squadron of Hurricanes that was shortly to arrive there. Stories of Hurricanes were all we seemed to have at that time to boost our morale. There never seemed to be any mention of that beautiful air-

4

craft, the Spitfire. Anyway, anybody with half an eye could see that no amount of morale-boosting would make the slightest difference. The Japanese had caught us on the hop and were advancing absolutely as they wished at a rate that bewildered even themselves. So I found a berth on what was, I think, the next to last ship out of Singapore before the town fell. It was a decrepit little tub about 30 feet long, with a considerable list. A great number of women and children were on board and the decks were festooned with washing.

We set sail for Jakarta (Batavia) feeling that, even without any hindrance from the Japanese, there was not a very good chance of our arriving there. As we went out to sea we were joined by several cargo ships, including two oil tankers. We were not in a convoy: we were simply a party of ships without any protection whatever, which must be the most dangerous way of all for ships to travel in enemy waters.

Inevitably, we were spotted by the Japanese, who bombed the party when we were well out to sea. They set both tankers ablaze and hit all the other ships but us. I gave thought to how we would manage if hit because the number of lifeboats was hopelessly inadequate for the women and children on board. I spent several minutes thinking about dying, because that seemed the only possibility. Then, suddenly and surprisingly, the aircraft went away, leaving us the only ship unbombed. The only reason I can suggest for this is either that they were short of petrol or that we had such a list that they thought they had hit us already. We arrived without further incident in Jakarta. I have examined the cable I sent to Emmie, to check the date, it is rather smudged, but it is almost certainly 16 February.

Soon after my arrival in Jakarta, I was befriended by a Dutch family who took me to the biggest hotel there and bought me a rijstafel. One of the experiences a visitor was expected to have in Java, this consisted of an enormous meal which included almost every savoury food that this magnificent and fertile country had to offer, all mixed up together, whether egg, fish, meat or vegetable, topped by all manner of sauces and borne in by a line of waiters. Advice about the sauces was necessary because some of them, made from the smallest chillies, known as *lombok*, were fiery hot to an untrained English palate. The name of the dish, *rijstafel*, comes from the fact that beneath all this, as a first layer, was boiled rice. In the native diet, the savoury things are simply garnishings for the rice: in the Dutch version, they really became the whole meal. One required three hours to eat the sort of *rijstafel* I was served at that hotel. Later, the extravagance of it was put clearly into perspective by many of my experiences, and I had reason to be ashamed.

After jakarta, I was not too well, not because of the *rijstafel*, but because of some tropical fever. We went to Cheribon in the north and for a short time to Tchilichap in the south, from which a party of 15 pregnant women left with an RAF padre on what was almost certainly the last ship out. I remember at the time wondering about the morality of a parson clearing out when it seemed highly probable that we would become prisoners of war – or worse – and the services of such men could be of value to us. And I was puzzled that a parson was necessary with a group of pregnant women, or, indeed, why any escort at all was needed. I had been impressed on many occasions by just how cool and effective women can be in these critical situations if left to their own devices. The party got away safely but we were bombed and raked by machine-gunfire in Tchilichap. These were days of utter confusion, with nobody in overall charge, no known plan and no organisation. I finished up with Donald MaGrath.

* * *

I had known Donald in England. A gentle cultured man, a man absolutely without guile, and with such a calmness in his voice that, later, even the Japanese, not understanding a word, detected it and he got away unharmed (according to a story, the truth of which I do not doubt) in a situation where any other officer might have been severely punished or even shot. Of this, more later. Donald concealed a most forceful personality beneath his bland manner – and he had a ready wit. A

6

most excellent man in any situation, but particularly this one. He was a pillar of strength to me until our ways parted some weeks later. We had met for the first time at RAF Mount Batten when he was in medical charge of the barrage balloon people over a wide area of south-west England; we met for the second time in a staff car in Java.

As I remember it, MaGrath was also charged, like me, with the duty of forming the medical service of an RAF squadron for the defence of Java. Singapore had by now fallen to the Japanese and the position in the whole of Indonesia was, to say the least, critical. We heard rumours that Java would fall without a struggle and, in fact, on 8 March it did. We were stopped in our staff car by a British service policeman who saluted and told us that the island had capitulated, so we were now prisoners of war and would we therefore kindly proceed to Tasik Malaja aerodrome. A thoroughly unreal, almost grotesque situation: we had been captured without even having set eyes on a Japanese soldier.

Some went to the south coast of the island to try to get away by boat. Almost nobody, so far as I know, succeeded; the difficulties were too great. Australia, many hundreds of miles away, was the possible objective, but I was told the wind and the currents did not favour this: they tended to take a boat across the Indian Ocean in the direction of South Africa, a journey of several thousand miles. Anybody who tried to conceal himself on the south coast, looking for a boat, was almost certain to be turned over to the Japanese and instant death (it turned out) because the local populace was extremely frightened – far too frightened to cooperate with Allied prisoners of war and, indeed, not much in a frame of mind to do so. The situation was totally different from that in Europe; the people had no reason that they could see to favour the Allies and, in any case, our white skins made us marked men. Rather naturally, they did not want their boats taken, so altogether we had no reason to expect to be popular. Some who did find boats, according to stories reaching us, got a short distance and capsized; some who got further were, so far as we knew, never heard of again; some even found their way back to the camp, which was well inland, having discovered the hopelessness of their attempts.

Clearly, the doctors could not try to get away. With a large number of Allied POWs, an unknown number of doctors and a future in the lap of the gods, but unlikely to be pleasant, the services of all the medical personnel would certainly be required throughout the coming imprisonment.

Tasik Malaja was an aerodrome with large metal hangars and several other smaller buildings and it was here that we set up our camp on the concrete floor – in considerable luxury, compared with our later experiences. Our hangar contained, so far as I recall, only officers. No sort of sanitary facilities existed on the scale required and I well remember Donald MaGrath and I, on the second or third day, going to the hangar and somebody shouting out 'When are you going to dig us a latrine, Doc?' What innocents they were. It also gives some idea of our degree of disorganisation. The answer was obvious: 'Spades are available and you will dig yourselves sufficient latrines before the day is out.' And so latrines were dug. The trouble, I suppose, was that, up to then, officers had not seen themselves in this sort of role. We had a good deal to learn.

We were a mixed lot. Two Wing Commanders, Gregson and Steadman, were the senior among us, Steadman being the Commanding Officer, or perhaps Senior British Officer would have been more accurate – the term gained currency later. I was to see a great deal of Gregson, and got to know him well as time passed. We had some money for official spending and we settled down into a sort of routine, obtaining our rations by purchase from the local populace, who were not slow to realise the possibilities for a little quick profit. Indeed, besides supplying our needs officially, they congregated round the camp perimeter selling their wares in a private capacity, both food and other more personal services being offered by the young women who cried, '*Mack-mack*' all day at the boundary fence. The meaning of the term was quite evident. Almost onomatopoeic.

Camp duties and sanitary chores were now carried out more

or less willingly by the officers – and Gregson had a way with the unwilling. Daily sick parades were held, though we did not have a great deal of sickness during these first few days. Besides MaGrath and myself, Alastair Forbes, a doctor from Aberdeen, was with us. We had to look ahead to decide as far as possible what medical and non-medical supplies we would need and make an attempt to obtain them. I therefore took an ambulance, having drawn some money from the camp funds, and went to any town that I could reach, buying what medicines I could, and because they might come in useful, all the paper and pencils I could lay my hands on – and a few paint-boxes and brushes (which were of Japanese origin, some of the paints, I discovered, being highly toxic). We kept clean by bathing in the torrential rain that fell each afternoon at about 4 o'clock, simply standing under the eaves with a piece of soap.

In those early innocent days, we devised various activities for ourselves. We had language classes; we even arranged a concert party, partly because it was considered to be the done thing among prisoners in the First World War and we had some veterans of that war with us. It was all a novel experience: some kidded themselves (all of us to some extent, I suppose) that it was all a bit of a joke – and none of us had yet seen a Jap. How green we were was revealed by the innocence of the songs in the revue that was being rehearsed:

> Oh! We are the officers' working party,
> Not very hale but we're terribly hearty;
> When there's work to be done, we're on the spot,
> We're not so energetic, but we're terribly hot.
>
> Navvies, mates and garden-weeders
> Wing Commanders and Squadron Leaders
> We've no time for languages, Malay or German,
> We kill all the flies and exterminate the vermin.

And so on, verse after guileless verse. One song even contained the lines:

And when we get back home again to Blighty,
We're sure to shoot a line about our stay.

How very little did we know.

After three weeks, we saw the Japanese for the first time. They inspected us (with considerable curiosity), took Wing Commander Steadman away and shot him. It was said – probably with truth, but we were not to know – that they shot him because, when questioned, he gave only the information required by the Geneva Convention: the names, numbers, ranks and units of his men. One can well assume that the Japanese required more; he would not give it, so they killed him. But I think there was, in addition, another reason as I saw similar behaviour later on. Faced with a group of prisoners, the Japanese, perhaps to some extent afraid of them, sought to deprive them of their leadership, either in the brutal manner they showed on this occasion or, as happened later when we were off to Haruku, by humiliating the Senior British Officer in front of his men, beating him unmercifully. We were to learn that gentlemanly behaviour was not part of the training of Japanese troops.

The performance of the concert party took place not long after the Japanese arrival. They attended. In the light of the disappearance of Steadman – we did not then know his fate – their presence, occupying the first two rows of chairs in the audience, made the whole thing seem very hollow and, to me, at any rate, most embarrassing. We revealed far too much about ourselves.

* * *

We left Tasik Malaja. The party split up and I parted company with Donald MaGrath and Alastair Forbes. It was soon afterwards, though I am not quite sure of the precise details, that Donald demonstrated his remarkable capacity for keeping out of trouble simply by force of personality. He became separated from his party in some manner on the way to Bandung and was picked up by the Japanese. Anybody else

10

would have immediately been accused of trying to escape, with dire results, but not so MaGrath. There was, no doubt, a good deal of shouting on the part of the Japanese, but I feel quite sure that he gave a level-headed explanation of his predicament, gently, softly and with a flicker of a smile on his face – but in an entirely incomprehensible language to the Japanese. We kept out of serious trouble. I think he was arrested and kept in the guardroom for some time but emerged unscathed. Not for nothing was he a psychiatrist in peacetime. He seemed incapable of thinking ill of any man. (He has since confirmed this story.)

Leaving Tasik Malaja, we had our first acquaintance with the order 'All men take only what they can carry' – a totally novel order, but the shape of things to come: we were to hear it many times. As this had been our first camp and we had arrived there by some sort of transport, we all had a considerable number of material possessions with us. Before one has experienced real hardship, such things are difficult to give up. The supplies of medicine such as we had (Forbes had taken a half-share) were taken by transport, but each man could only take for himself what he could put on his back. We were to learn that moves would always be at short notice and that we would be given very little detail, but we understood that we were to go to the railway station about two miles away, marching, of course.

We knew little of our capacity to carry things, but we were soon to find out – and to decide what was valuable to take and what to leave behind. Monetary worth did not enter it later, but at this stage, unstarved and unacquainted with the full brutality of the Japanese, we thought that valuable possessions were still valuable possessions. Men arranged ambitious devices to increase their capacity to carry their belongings, or so they thought – two poles slung between the shoulders of two men with both their loads in the middle, or one pole on the shoulder with a load at each end. Indonesian-style. Many of these ideas came to nought: we, unpractised at carrying loads, learned the hard way that if you start off with too much, you have to leave most of it somewhere on the road-

11

side, much more than if you had been more selective at first, simply because a smaller, well-packed load is so much less tiring. The Indonesian method of a pole with a load at each end carried on the shoulder is perfect in the hands of experts – skinny little men carrying prodigious amounts – but it depends for its success on the pole being springy and the load bouncing up and down in time with the gait of the bearer, thus intermittently relieving the weight on the shoulder, part of which, anyway, is borne by the hand holding the pole just in front of its centre. It will not work when you march, only when you trot in the characteristic toe-to-heal trot of Indonesian manner. No wonder the Malay for 'trot' is *jalan-jalan* – most descriptive.

The best way to arrange things, we learned from experience, was to make two loads, the larger containing the absolutely essential things, and the smaller, the non-essential but desirable things. Anything that was simply valuable for its own sake (cameras, binoculars) was better thrown away at once. Blanket, mosquito net, what clothes I had, two alloy dishes, knife, spoon and fork, soap, toothbrush, razor and a photograph of Emmie were for me the essential things. My second package contained one or two books, some paper and paints and a few other odds and ends. I managed always to bring both along. Nothing else was valuable enough to take. Everything, of course, depended on how far we had to go (though we were never told in advance), but the two-mile journey from Tasik Malaja aerodrome to the station was our baptism and stripped us of much unnecessary gear. The Javanese population no doubt derived some benefit from what we left behind and what we discarded on the roadside.

We arrived at Surabaya in May 1942 and were accommodated in a large brick-built camp which had probably been a school. It was already occupied by prisoners of war, mainly Dutch, and an effective camp routine had been established. We lived in reasonable comfort: many of us slept on the floor, but that did not matter; it was at least dry, which is more than one can say of many of our later beds, and we were not overcrowded. The food, by all the standards we were later to experience, was adequate, mainly rice and beans, the rice being sometimes unpolished – so-called red rice, pleasant to eat, but rare. More usually, we had white rice, that is, polished rice, which can be dangerous stuff. The reason for this, as I think is fairly generally known, is that the process of polishing removes the outer layer which contains vitamins of the 'B' group, without which, serious – and eventually fatal – illness develops. White rice must therefore always be eaten with other foods which supply these essential nutrients. Of this, unhappily, I shall say much more later.

Though our diet was adequate at this time, there was a certain sameness about it and in these early days, before we had much acquaintance with privation, these things mattered. A senior colleague decided that he needed some bacon. He obtained illicitly, and I have no doubt, at great expense, about a pound of it from an outside source. (Being quartered in a town, the Dutch going out on working parties could make contacts to enable a certain amount of extra food to be brought in.) The bacon was my colleague's chief topic of conversation for several days before it arrived and finally, one evening, it came, well-dried and in good order. Perhaps overcome by enthusiasm, the owner of the bacon decided it would taste better if rather more moist and less salt. It was to be started next day at breakfast, so he put it in a bath of water overnight to leach out some of the salt. What he had forgotten (and what he should have known, but he was an administrative doctor) was that this was the tropics and bacteria work fast. So long as the bacon was sufficiently salt, it was safe, but the moment the salt was diluted, the micro-organism took charge. I lived in the same room (though somehow understood that I was not to share in the bacon) and, waking in the night, noticed a strong smell of corruption. By morning, the whole room stank. There was no hope of eating the bacon and we were all relieved to see it thrown away. It made a very good joke for several days, particularly among those who were not to share it, the chief character being rather pompous and a proper butt for humour, and the camp fairly resounded with laughter. But it was a dreadful waste of bacon.

For some reason no doubt connected with the bathing facilities, we found ourselves with a near-epidemic of ear infection. It affected the external ear – the part outside the eardrum – and was fungal in origin and extremely painful. I did not suffer, but one only had to see a man with it to know what he was going through. I found a treatment which worked, though I cannot now remember whether by trial and error or as the result of advice from colleagues more experienced in tropical medicine than I. This involved meticulous cleaning of the ear with cotton wool on sticks (we still had such things) and then treatment with icthyol (a coal tar derivative), mercurochrome and alcohol, each in a two-day course, the whole treatment lasting six days. The cleaning was the most essential part and excruciatingly painful, every particle of fungus having to be removed. The men stood up to the pain well, as the condition itself allowed no sleep and relief was rapid. Fortunately, it worked every time. One difficulty was that I did not have an ear-mirror – the round mirror that is worn on a headband – nor a torch, nor any ear specula – the conical metal tubes that are put into the ear to enable one to get a better view. But I did have a woman's handbag mirror and I found that with this, held at an angle near my eye so that it caught the sunlight and directed it at the ear, I could get a look down – and then I did the cleaning from memory, alternately inspecting and cleaning. It was much easier than one might think and most satisfying, because a man strained and sleepless when he first came was transformed into a cheerful ordinary chap by the second day. These clinics became so large that at one time I was seeing between 20 and 30 patients in a morning.

One of my lasting memories of this camp was of the beauty of the Dutch bugle calls for waking, lights out and all the rest of the daily occasions. The bugler was an artist (and knew it); Dutch bugle calls are good to hear anyway and he put in his own variations. Possibly, he played a trumpet rather than a bugle, which is rather a limiting instrument. It is perhaps strange that such an apparently minor matter should have given me so much pleasure, but it did, and I expect it pleased many other people as well.

14

The other memorable thing that happened at this camp was that I carved my kingfisher. The wood burned in Javanese railway engines at that time – and in our cookhouse – was so-called bastard teak, a knotty, curly-grained, very hard teak, useless for any other purpose. I managed to get hold of a piece, found myself a hacksaw-blade, ground it into a knife-blade on a building stone and spent many a happy and emblistered hour whittling out the effigy of an ordinary European kingfisher to keep me company. I painted it with some of the water-colours I had bought at Tasik Malaja, gave myself a sharp attack of lead poisoning through licking my brush, and managed to keep it, finally bringing it home. It became one of my talisman possessions (a matter I will touch on later) and I think I partly owe my life to it.

2

HIPPOCRATES GO HANG

Before we had been very long at Surabaya, the Japanese ordered a working party to go to Semarang on the north coast of Java to extend the airport runway there. This was clearly for military purposes and it was therefore contrary to the terms of the Geneva Convention for prisoners of war to do this work, but the Japanese paid no heed to this: either you did what you were told or, as had already been demonstrated to us, you were killed. As far as I know, all the work done by Allied prisoners of war for the Japanese anywhere in their sphere of operations was of military use to them, be it the Burma–Thailand railway, the Semarang airport or our later work at Haruku and Ambon. The Japanese were not signatories to the Geneva Convention; we were.*

Wing Commander Gregson was Senior Officer in the party and I was their doctor. Gregson was to prove himself quite admirable in dealing with the Japanese: he had no fear of them and many of them were a little in awe of him – or so it appeared. He was an ardent theosophist and, while I do not claim to understand his beliefs, they undoubtedly gave him great strength. The party consisted of 200 British with three other British officers. In the same camp were 100 Dutch with their own officers and a young Dutch doctor. We did not mix very much and the story I tell is of the 200 British.

---

*Japan did sign the 1929 Convention but refused to ratify it. They treated it, except towards the end, with callous and brutal disregard.

16

We were housed in two large *atap* huts close to the airport runway. (*Atap* is a light palm-leaf construction, arranged like thatch, supported on a bamboo framework tied together with long strands of vegetable fibre. It keeps the rain out and lets the air circulate, so is ideal in a continuously warm climate, even one with a high rainfall.) The view was wide; we were close to the seashore and all around the airport – and around us – were ditches where mosquitoes bred and supported a vast number of tiny fish, which in their turn were caught by marvellously coloured small kingfishers. The surviving mosquitoes bit us and gave us malaria. Clearly, the whole place was a fairly recently drained swamp. We had mosquito nets, but mosquito nets, after all, are only useful when you are inside them, and though the men all slept in their nets, the evenings, before they went to bed, were the dangerous time. During our stay at Semarang about three-quarters of our company went down with malaria at some time, but fortunately it was of benign tertian type, which does not usually kill and, in fact, killed none of us. We were officially given precious little in the way of medical supplies, but more of that later.

The Japanese guard, some 15 of them under a lieutenant, lived in a small brick building outside the gate of our camp. They supervised the work on the runway and counted us every morning and evening, making us number in Japanese to commands in Japanese from our British officers. There were always a few men who were too ill with malaria to come on parade. We had no thermometers or other clinical apparatus, except my stethoscope, so the only way to check a man's temperature was to feel his skin, and such was the overcrowding that the only part of him that I could reasonably get at when he lay on his mat was his feet. One became very skilled at judging the temperature by applying the back of the hand to the sole of a patient's foot, and each evening, before the parade, I had to assess which of the new patients with malaria were unfit to go out. When I had made my decision – in which I always had the greatest cooperation from the patients concerned – those who could stand on parade did so and those who were too bad lay on their mats. I would report the number of sick, the Japanese guard in charge would argue but finally count the bodies in bed and feel the soles of their feet – and we usually got away without further trouble.

I had more cooperation from the guard than I otherwise would have done because, by a great stroke of good fortune, I was able to blackmail them. All of them had fought in the Sino–Japanese War – a dismal, almost-forgotten struggle in which the Japanese invaded and tried to capture parts of China before the Second World War. The Chinese were no fools, being rather clever at what might be called passive warfare, and saw to it that any Japanese who wanted to take home a little loot in the form of a golden tooth or two had his golden caps put over carious teeth with inevitable trouble later, and also – and very important to us – that every Chinese prostitute associating with the Japanese had gonorrhoea. The consequence, apart from toothache, was that all our guards, bar one, suffered from gonorrhoea in a chronic and long-standing form. They were entirely untreated, which is hardly surprising because the Japanese Army at that time treated any form of venereal disease by sending the sufferer to the nearest fighting. Our guards, contrary perhaps to the popular notion that Japanese soldiers are aching to die for their country, knew a soft job when they had it and were therefore reluctant to report sick. So I was a godsend to them – a prisoner doctor who presumably knew something about treating gonorrhoea. No knowledge on my part was really necessary because, for some reason I could never fathom, in those days before penicillin and all the later antibiotics, they all insisted on one form of treatment: the injection into a vein of steadily increasing doses of trypaflavine, an orange dye, on alternate days.

I never knew the treatment do anybody any good – nor did I expect it, their disease was too chronic – and perhaps I might be criticised on ethical grounds for accommodating the guards, but I had very little choice as no treatment I could carry out in the camp would do any better. In fact, it turned out immensely to our advantage. The procedure was always the same: there would be a tug at my mosquito net at dead of night and when I had woken up sufficiently, the consultation would take place – I will not go into detail – by the light of a torch. The conversation that followed, carried out in a mixture of Malay, Japanese and sign, hardly varied. 'I will treat you,' I said, 'but I only have enough medicine to start, so I must go to the hospital to collect some more.' They were not allowed to report sick to me, which is why the whole thing took place secretly.

Now the hospital, at Semarang, about two miles away, had been very well stocked with medical supplies by the provident Dutch. It was Japanese policy to replace the Dutch medical staff with Javanese doctors (their slogans 'Asia for the Asians' and *Bangoen Asia* – 'Asia Awake' – were emblazoned all over the town on enormous posters), but rather Germanically perhaps, they made no replacement if they could not find a Javanese doctor in a particular speciality, so the Dutch pharmacist – a magnificent man called Blomberg – remained in his job. He was a great mountain of a man and joked that his name meant that he was the flower on the mountain. Always, the morning after I had had a night-time consultation with a Japanese patient, a lorry would be driven into the camp with the patient as driver or escort. I would be made to lie on the floor so as to be invisible from the pavements and we would go to the hospital to visit Dr Blomberg. Once we were there, the Japanese guard, being my illicit patient, was hardly in a position to complain, whatever I did, and I was able, with Blomberg's admirable assistance, to take into the camp all the medical supplies we needed – including the trypaflavine for the guard and a few extra phials to start the same routine with the inevitable next patient.

As we became more practised, we did not stop at medicines; we took in shoes, books, money, cigarettes, a gramophone and records. These Blomberg begged from his friends in the town who were not yet interned. In this way, I obtained a fine pair of ski-boots which shod me for a long time. And we came by a marvellous lute (clearly, a most valuable instrument) which we somehow managed to string and which we cherished as there was always somebody who could strum out a tune on the guitar – and the lute sounded so much better. Later, as we moved from camp to camp, we kept losing sight of this lute, but it always turned up again. Because of this piece of blackmail – for it was no less – we were probably one of the healthiest camps in the Far East, notwithstanding our malaria. It is difficult, if one is honest, to transfer the ethics outlined in the Hippocratic oath to the extraordinary situation in which I found myself; anyway, whatever the reader may think, I took advantage of the situation most outrageously, knowing that my guard felt, as my patient, that he would be wiser to turn a blind eye to what was going on and was probably aware that if he made a fuss, the reason for my visit to the hospital might come to light, much to his detriment – and incidentally, mine.

Blomberg and I began to introduce refinements to the routine. One good one was to prepare a drink for the guard, consisting of syrup of orange, absolute alcohol and water. These Japanese were simple country people and a potion like this would bring on almost immediate sleep every time, which left Blomberg and me free to discuss the latest news. Here, I have a minor criticism: his news was always good and never true; perhaps he wanted to keep our spirits high. These visits went on for fully six months at the rate of about two a week – the guards were a shifting population and, for all I knew, their friends from the Japanese garrison in the town also took advantage of the service.

All this came to a sudden end. One day the Japanese guard called me to the guardroom and showed me the phone off the hook. I picked it up and a voice I did not recognise, clearly Dutch, told me that I would be in danger if I went to the hospital again – a most mysterious telephone call. I shall never understand how the caller persuaded the authorities, let alone the guards, to allow it to come through to me.

We only remained in Semarang another month and I had enough medical supplies in stock, but naturally I was most concerned over what might have happened to Blomberg. I went to the Japanese CO – a new one – and told him I needed lime to kill the fly larvae in the latrine because they were a danger not only to us but to the Japanese, and I needed to collect it at the hospital. He was most reluctant to let me go

20

but finally agreed and accompanied me himself. Clearly, he had his suspicions, because every container was opened and its contents spilled out on to the floor before I was allowed to take it back to the camp. But the important thing was that Blomberg was still there, though conversation was not allowed. I do not know the final fate of this amusing, courageous man, but we all owed him a deep debt of gratitude. Not one man died in that camp, which left me very clear in my mind about the value of gentle blackmail, whatever Hippocrates may say.

The one guard who never sought my ministrations was, unfortunately, the only one who stayed throughout our time. He probably knew what was going on, he was always a thorn in my flesh and beat me when the occasion arose. The whole system nearly came to light when a Japanese sergeant whom I had treated gradually started to become deeply pigmented, resembling a Javanese rather than a Japanese. I was puzzled, but said nothing. He suddenly disappeared, which was not entirely unusual as the guard changed throughout our time, but I was told afterwards that, as I was using trypaflavine, he concluded that it must be good and thought he would get a better cure if he had a more intensive course. So on the alternate days when I did not give him an injection, he went and got one from a Japanese medical orderly. Whether this caused his pigmentation I shall never know, but it appeared that his disease was discovered because he was going to the Japanese orderly – and he was dispatched to the nearest fighting. Our lives hung by threads in those days.

Food was not a major preoccupation at Semarang. The rations provided by the Japanese were not lavish, but we managed. We had a slight additional advantage: each day, at about midday, when the men came back to camp for their meal, women from the neighbouring villages came to the perimeter fence with all manner of foodstuffs for sale. Because of the gifts of money we had received through Dr Blomberg, we were able to buy some of these things, though we had to be very careful because many of the dishes offered for sale were concoctions of rice, meat and chillies, already cooked and wrapped in banana leaves. These were most palatable but

21

undoubtedly were heavily infected with all manner of danger-ous bacteria, particularly of the dysentery and typhoid groups. So I placed an absolute embargo on buying cooked foods and so far as I know, Wing Commander Gregson being a man of strong personality, capable of obtaining not only absolute obedience but intense loyalty from his men, this order was not disobeyed. Certainly, we had no cases of dysentery or the typhoid group of diseases at Semarang. The things we could buy safely were fruit, which could be washed and skinned, spice such as curry powder and chillies, vegetables which had to be cooked, and sugar. These additions enabled us to have much more varied meals than we would have managed with just rice, vegetables, salt, coconut oil and a little meat. In my recollection, the high spot of our cuisine at Semarang was a dish we had one night of curried heron.

Being able to buy goods at the barbed wire had one very interesting consequence. One day I laid in a fairly large stock of sugar, called *Gula Java* for the camp. It was dark brown, in the form of solid discs, each a few inches across. It always contained the dead bodies of insects trapped in it while it was solidifying, but sugar, after all, is an excellent preservative, capable, when highly concentrated, of inhibiting the growth of any dangerous bacteria, so the only disadvantage of the insects was one of elegance – and the need for elegance is inversely proportional to hunger. The sugar that I bought was wrapped, each disc in a separate piece of paper, and when I unwrapped it, I found that my suppliers had come by an up-to-date American textbook of surgery, and had, moreover, used con-secutive pages as wrappers. After undoing the whole of my purchase, I found that I had a complete chapter on the opera-tion of cineplasty (or kinoplasty), a technique of making tunnels in the muscles remaining in an arm after the hand had been amputated so that they could be used to actuate an articulated artificial hand – a method with which I was unfa-miliar. This was the only medical reading matter that I had had for a year and I read it avidly and remembered it all, gaining some knowledge that was to be useful to me later on when we returned to Surabaya.

The work for which we had been brought to Semarang was, as I have said, the extension of the runway at the airport. As we were living in the hangars, it was almost on our doorstep. The tempo of the work was as slow as the men could make it without actually incurring the wrath of the Japanese guard, and various devices could be used to sabotage it as it went on. Coconuts were fairly easy to buy at the perimeter fence and the men saw to it that as the work proceeded they were planted beneath the runway in the hope that when they sprouted, they would split the concrete, which, by today's standards, was thin. A good number of the guards' brassbound poles, used to chastise us, also found their way beneath the concrete.

The Japanese have a remarkable talent for making do. Our work required a trainload of hardcore, sand and cement to be brought from the town. There was a siding near our hangars and therefore bringing these materials to the edge of the airport was not difficult, but there was still about a quarter-mile to go to the site. The Japanese decided to take the load there by train, so they made our men tear up an existing unused track and re-lay it across the grass, sleepers and all, but with no attempt to lay it level and without ballast. The ground was marshy. When the great day came to take the train across, we expected (and hoped) that the track would subside, and the train tip over and make an almighty mess, but we were sorely disappointed. The train rocked like a ship on the high seas as it went across the uneven marshy ground, but apart from this it went without a hitch. Had we British had to arrange the operation there would have been a survey, ballast-laying and all manner of precautions against disaster, and I am sure that if we had cut our corners as the Japanese did, the whole thing would have been a fiasco. But this does show something about the Japanese character and, I think, about ours, and perhaps indicates one reason why they had such phenomenal early success in their campaign – and possibly also why we lost so heavily at that time.

Our men worked a long day, from early morning until dusk, with a short time off for their midday meal, which was rice and vegetables. When they came back to the camp in the

23

evening, there was time for a wash, the sick parade, the parade (*tenko*) to be counted by the Japanese and then the evening meal, which we tried to make as good as provisions would allow. After the meal, there was nothing but talk and our illicit gramophone until bedtime. For much of the time, we only had three records – Deanna Durbin singing a piece from *The Maids of Cadiz*, a romantic ditty called 'How I love the kisses of Dolores', and a strange song with little to commend it entitled 'When I put on my long white robe' – one could never decide whether this was meant to be religious or faintly funny. Anyway, the singer 'looked so fine, felt so good, when he put on his long white robe', and the chorus was a mass of 'Allelujahs'. Curiously, I cannot remember what was on the reverse side of any of these records. We had a principle which, I believe, enormously improved our spirit – we dressed for dinner. None of us had much in the way of spare clothes, though these were luxurious times compared with what was to come, and while there was something to change into, we cleaned up and changed in the evening. Few things did more to boost our morale.

The incessant gramophone was not sufficient to amuse us, and though we had a few books, we had little light. So I decided that it might be a good idea to arrange one light strong enough to read by and to read aloud to anyone who wanted to listen. By good fortune, we had a *Complete Short Stories of O Henry*, which was ideally suited to the occasion – light, funny, romantic, and dealing with completely human situations, albeit with an American flavour. It was quite a moving experience to sit reading to an audience of perhaps 20 men, discernible in the darkness. O Henry served us well: when we had gone right through him once, I read several of his stories a second time.

We had, of course, had no communication with home, and the distribution of Red Cross parcels was not for us (in fact, we each received our one and only half-parcel in 1945, a little before the end). There was great rejoicing, therefore, when we were told that we would be allowed to send a postcard home at Christmas 1942. These were handed out to us with the instruction to choose three of a selection of standard phrases and then add 20 words of our own. Some of the set phrases were not very appropriate, such as: 'I am well, so do not worry me'. The cards were handed back to the Japanese and, as far as I know, the majority did not arrive, but mine was an exception. It was picked up by a shepherd in Ireland, charred, but with the address still clearly legible. He, out of the goodness of his heart – he cannot have had much money to spare – sent it in an envelope to Mother's home at Radlett (where I had addressed it) and it arrived on 23 August 1943, 8 months after it was posted (and 11 days after Emmie had been notified that I was a prisoner – I had been posted missing for 17 months). Mother redirected it, unread, to Emmie, who was living and working at the time in Devon. It caught the 5.30 post from Radlett. The message was:

2. I am now in a Japanese Prisoner-of-War camp in Java.

3. My health is excellent.

10. I am constantly thinking of you. It will be wonderful when we meet again.

    Take care of yourself, my Darling Emmie. Be Happy. Give my love to Mother and everybody. God bless you.
    Dick

It turned out that the aircraft bearing the mail had crashed and caught fire in Ireland. Presumably, most of the letters had been destroyed.

To return to the story of Semarang. In this camp, near to the town, stray dogs were a problem. They gravitated to us and nobody could blame the men for making pets of them – there were precious little other outlet for affection. But dogs, particularly strays, are a menace in the tropics as they carry intestinal parasites, and our washing facilities, though adequate, as we had piped water, were not lavish; so, again with remarkable cooperation from the men, I had every so often to have a drive against the strays. One could not ask for the help

25

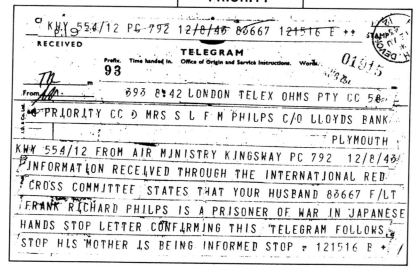

KWY 554/12 PC 792 12/8/43 83667 121516 E ++

RECEIVED

TELEGRAM

Prefix.　Time handed in.　Office of Origin and Service Instructions.　Words.

93

01915

From

393 8.42 LONDON TELEX OHMS PTY CC 58

PRIORITY CC D MRS S L F M PHILPS C/O LLOYDS BANK

PLYMOUTH

KWY 554/12 FROM AIR MINISTRY KINGSWAY PC 792 12/8/43
INFORMATION RECEIVED THROUGH THE INTERNATIONAL RED
CROSS COMMITTEE STATES THAT YOUR HUSBAND 83667 F/LT
FRANK RICHARD PHILPS IS A PRISONER OF WAR IN JAPANESE
HANDS STOP LETTER CONFIRMING THIS TELEGRAM FOLLOWS
STOP HIS MOTHER IS BEING INFORMED STOP = 121516 E +

A photocopy of the cable received by Emmie on August 12th, 1943 after I
had been missing for one year five months (and a few days).

26

GERRARD 9234
Tel. Extn. 3803.

Any communications on the
subject of this letter
should be addressed to:-

THE
UNDER SECRETARY OF STATE,
AIR MINISTRY,
and the following number
quoted:- P. 369744/43/P4/B3.

AIR MINISTRY,
(Casualty Branch),
73-77 Oxford Street,
LONDON, W.1.

12ᵗʰ Aug: 1943

~~Sir~~,
Madam,

I am directed to confirm a telegram from
this department in which you were notified that
information has now been received through the
International Red Cross Committee, stating that
your *HUSBAND 83667 F Lᵗ.*
Frank Richard Philps.
Royal Air Force, is a prisoner of war.

The Committee's report quotes Japanese
information and states that he is at a
Java Camp   . He should
now be able to communicate with you.

A pamphlet regarding communications with
prisoners of war is enclosed as it may be of
service to you.

I am, ~~Sir~~,
Madam,
Your obedient Servant,

Mrs Philps.

for **Director** of Personal Services.
A. 2076.

The notification from the International Red Cross via the Air Ministry,
more than one year and five months after the event, that I was a prisoner of
war.

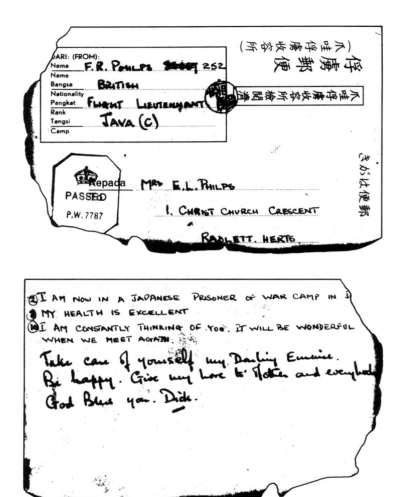

The postcard I sent to Emmie at Christmas 1942. It was the only act of mercy the Japanese showed us throughout the whole time. The aircraft carrying it crashed in Ireland and caught fire. I do not know the fate of the crew but a shepherd picked this up and forwarded it as an act of kindness.

WAR ORGANISATION
OF THE

PW/FE/1A/43.

BRITISH RED CROSS SOCIETY and ORDER OF ST. JOHN OF JERUSALEM

President:		*Grand Prior:*
HER MAJESTY THE QUEEN.		H.R.H. THE DUKE OF GLOUCESTER, K.G.

PRISONERS OF WAR DEPARTMENT

Chairman:
MAJOR-GENERAL SIR RICHARD HOWARD-VYSE, K.C.M.G., D.S.O.

Deputy Chairman:
J. M. EDDY, C.B.E.

TELEPHONE No.:
REGENT 0111 (5 LINES)

FAR EAST SECTION.
Controller: S. G. KING

9, PARK PLACE,
ST. JAMES'S STREET,
LONDON. S.W.1

When replying please quote reference: FE/38943.

17. 11. 43.

F/Lt. Frank Richard Philps. R.A.F.

Dear Mr Philps

      We have been officially advised that the above is a
prisoner of war in Japanese hands. We are very glad that this news
of his safety has been received.

      Letters and postcards, which must be limited to 25 words
not including addresses, may be sent post free to the prisoner.
They should be posted in the ordinary way, and not sent to us for
onward transmission. Letters should preferably be typewritten, or
alternatively they must be written in block capitals. Only relatives
and close friends should write, and in present circumstances no object
will be served by any one family writing more than once a fortnight.
The name and address of the sender must be written on the back of
the envelope. (Members of H.M. Forces should give a civilian address
of a relative or friend who would be willing to forward replies.) No
enclosures whatever, even photographs, are allowed, nor may homemade
envelopes or economy labels be used. No reference to Naval, Military,
Aerial, Economic or Political matters is permitted.

      Your attention is also drawn to the attached leaflet giving
particulars of the facilities that we are able to offer for the typing
of letters.

      You will find at the end of this letter the exact method of
address that you should use when writing to your prisoner.

/Parcels

Parcels cannot at present be sent owing to the refusal of the Japanese to grant safe conducts for the ships that would have to be utilised for such a parcels service. Every endeavour is being made to secure a change in their present attitude and if, as a result of these efforts, facilities are accorded, the next-of-kin will be advised. Full details will also be published in the Press.

This Organisation, in collaboration with other national Red Cross Societies, is meanwhile doing everything possible to help Far East prisoners by providing food, medicines, clothing and other supplies. Already several thousand tons of such supplies have been shipped to the Far East, and distributed equally among all prisoners of Allied nationality in Japanese hands. Plans have been made, and continue to be made, for the supplementing of these supplies by further despatches and by local purchases in the Far East.

We should like you to know that we shall retain complete records of the prisoner at this office, and shall be only too pleased to render you all assistance. If you write or call please be sure to quote the reference at the head of this letter, as this will enable us to give you prompt attention.

P.S. Will you very kindly let us
know whether we are to take
our Lewdown address as permanent,
as we were given c/o Lloyds Bank, Plymouth
by the Air Ministry & A.G.
We are so glad you have had a card.

Yours sincerely,

A.G.
for Controller.

PRISONER OF WAR POST
SERVICE DES PRISONNIERS DE GUERRE

FLIGHT LIEUTENANT F.R.PHILPS-R.A.F.
BRITISH PRISONER OF WAR
JAVA CAMP.

30

of the Japanese in this, because there was a distinct possibility that they would do nothing, or worse, would be cruel, so I had to do the job myself. I found that if a dog was docile, it was the simplest possible thing to kill it quite painlessly with a chair-leg. One simply stood beside it, behind the head, rested the lower jaw on the left hand and gave it a smart blow along the length of the skull with the chair-leg. No dog that I killed in this way ever even whimpered; they all just dropped dead. It seemed a brutal thing to do, but these were brutal times and public health was at stake. The Japanese at a later camp demonstrated their method of killing dogs, which was put the unfortunate animal into a sack and jump on it, their peals of laughter mingling with the dog's screams, until it was dead.

After about seven months, the runway was finished. We, and our work, were due to be inspected by a visiting Japanese senior officer, but before this could happen, all the men had to go out on to the freshly completed runway and sweep it with small hand-brushes. All that they succeeded in doing was to make the dust into some sort of pattern, but clearly Japanese honour was satisfied. Perhaps more important, it amused our people; the work was light, the climate good and the idea of sweeping an airport runway with small hand-brushes touched something in the British sense of humour. When the sweeping was satisfactorily completed, the Japanese colonel – no less – came and we were lined up for him to make a speech. It was only afterwards that we were told that he had been speaking in English; it was impossible to discern this, but thinking back, one realised that the word 'stoppu' occurred many times. Evidently, he included the punctuation in his speech. It appeared that he was congratulating us because we had worked so well and we were given a glass of beer each. It was a strange fluid, quite unrecognisable. Little did he know that beneath the runway were planted the makings of a coconut grove. We never learned whether they germinated and cracked the concrete.

We left Semarang early in 1943, about ten months after we were captured. Though it is difficult to enjoy any situation involving the loss of freedom, in a sense, and particularly in comparison with other camps we were later to occupy, I found the life in the Semarang camp bearable. One was not preoccupied with starvation, medical supplies were available to treat the men so that they remained relatively healthy in spite of malarial attacks, and we were in a beautiful place. The views across the airport were wide, magnificent egrets were always about the sky and kingfishers fished in the ditches. Above all, there was corporate spirit in the camp the like of which I have never seen before or since. This was almost entirely due to Gregson, a man, himself risen from the ranks, who understood men. Occasionally vicious, but seldom without reason, given to castigating anybody behaving foolishly (particularly officers), able to get his way by sheer force of personality ('make 'em frightened to do wrong'), sympathetic to the lower ranks, particularly those whom he knew had had a poor home – and he knew his men – utterly courageous, capable of diminishing a Japanese by the power of his will, this man won the loyalty and, to this day, the affection of the men at Semarang, who have never forgotten him.

Gregson was alert to the necessity of having some plan of mass escape, should the occasion arise. There were two Israeli airmen POWs who spoke a language which nobody in Java was likely to be able to understand, virtually, therefore, in code. Gregson's scheme made great and ingenious use of these two airmen, but unfortunately there was no opportunity to put it into action.

We returned to Surabaya. It is an engaging thought that the activities of a group of Chinese prostitutes in the late 1930s were to a great measure responsible for the survival in a reasonable state of health of all our men at Semarang. But for them, we should certainly have been short of medical supplies.

* * *

We found that at Surabaya the prisoners had not fared quite so well as we had. There had been 18 deaths among the several thousand there and they had an outbreak of dysentery in the camp. As might have been expected, the Roman Catholic priest and the Salvation Army personnel had rolled up their sleeves at the first sign of the outbreak and become nurses. This merely confirmed something that I had already learned, that in a sticky situation, particularly one requiring courage, members of the Salvation Army can be a tower of strength. At one stage, early on, we were inside the wire and several Dutch Salvation Army officers were outside, not yet having been interned. Each night at least one of them came, at considerable personal risk of being shot, and brought essential supplies to us. Ever since, I have been filled with admiration for Salvation Army personnel.

There was a man in the camp at Surabaya, a British soldier or airman, I do not now remember which as the differences became blurred, who had lost his left hand in a detonator explosion. It immediately struck me that here was an opportunity to use the knowledge that I had gained from reading the sugar wrappings at Semarang and I discussed it with him. He was most enthusiastic, so we decided to try to make him a functioning artificial hand. Firstly, I set about fashioning the hand, ably helped by a man named Scott who, before the war, had been a maintenance engineer in a soft drinks factory. If we succeeded in making the hand, I had sufficient local anaesthetic to operate on the man, but, obviously, we first had to see that we could make a useful hand with the materials available. We had aluminium alloy from broken-down machinery, some leather, a few screws and nails and some plaster of Paris. We had the tools to cut screw threads. We needed to melt the aluminium, and for this we had, as a cauldron, an old cast-iron lavatory cistern. I made a plaster cast of my left hand with the fingers half-way bent so that my thumb met the tip of my index finger (and had great difficulty in getting it off). Having winkled myself out of it, I pared the plaster down so that the index and middle fingers became a hook. I cut off the effigy of my fourth and little fingers from the cast. Scott and I then melted the aluminium in our cistern to cast the 'hand' in a sand mould made from my plaster of Paris effigy. I cannot now remember how we obtained the intense heat necessary, but our fuel was probably wood. I do remember that we had

33

some anxious moments wondering whether the stuff was going to melt at all. Having made the cast (first time lucky), Scott spent a couple of days hollowing it out with a drill and a file to make it lighter. The thumb was cast separately and was made to move by fashioning a strong hinge at its base and, in addition, the thumb was fixed on by a screw-thread so that it could be unscrewed and removed when only the hook was required. Inset into the two surfaces, on the thumb and fore-finger-hook, which met when the thumb was opposed, were rubber inlays to give a good grip. The thumb was made to work by the attachment of a piece of cord to a projection on the palmar surface near the base. This cord passed through a tunnel in the alloy at the 'wrist' and then passed up the arm. We made a leather 'sleeve', using our patient's forearm as our guide, fitting it tightly at the wrist and making it lace up to keep it on. It finished just below the elbow. We attached the hand to the sleeve with rivets we had made ourselves, and to our surprise it worked first time when we pulled the cord. The 'thumb' was made to return to its straightest position by a spring.

Obviously, if I was to operate on the patient to enable the hand to be worked by a muscle, we first had to be sure that his artificial hand was comfortable and worked sufficiently well to make the operation worth while, so he wore it for several weeks as a test. We found that with the thumb unscrewed, using the hook only, he could lift a weight of several pounds, and to my amazement, when walking round the camp one evening, I saw him playing cards – we still had a few grubby packs – holding his 'fan' of cards in his left hand, between the artificial thumb and forefinger. As what he was doing seemed impossible, I went closer and watched. he had tied the string, which was his 'tendon', to the back of his chair and was able, by carefully positioning his arm, to vary the tension on it with great precision, enabling him to hold his cards and to relax the grip sufficiently to remove one card at a time. Clearly, he had practised this carefully and was very proud of his achievement; more than likely, he had hoped that I would just happen along. From my point of view, it made the next stage well worth while. The operation went well – and the next day I was notified that I was to join a party of men leaving the camp to go on a working party. I left and did not see my patient again, though I had reports of him. He survived the war; but, untended, the tunnel I had made through the flexor muscles of his forearm that was to take the peg which would pull on the string 'tendon' to work his thumb, closed, and though he was no worse off as a result of my interference, the procedure was not given a chance to work. The hook, I was told, he found most useful throughout the rest of his imprisonment.

The working party was to go to the Moluccas – the Spice Islands – though, of course, we did not know this at the time. Now began a time which had a nightmare quality that makes some parts of it difficult to recall; indeed, up to this point in my life I have found the whole thing too painful to bring back to mind. Memory seems to suffer a block when one tries to take from it incidents which are better forgotten. The human mind is strange. The best parts, the funny parts, are remembered with ease; the ghastly parts require great effort. And also, days without incident at all slip into the limbo and are lost. So it is no accident that the following chapters give a more detailed account than those that have gone before. Also, I have notes made soon after my release to guide me.

3

HARUKU I. EPIDEMIC

I am aware that the next section of this story does not make pleasant reading, partly because of the brutality and ill-treatment it describes, but also because it is necessary to go into a considerable amount of very squalid medical detail. I have no choice: either the account is true, or it is useless and had better not have been written. I am fully aware of my responsibility to make it as accurate as a subjective statement can be. Although I kept a journal throughout the time, unfortunately I had to part with it on a subsequent sea journey. I wrote about our experiences soon after the war for a medical paper published in 1947[1] and since that time, the account has lain on a shelf, unread. I feel now that the reason for this is that I was quite unable to face reliving this time in any way. I have also avoided discussing it as I have found that stories oft repeated inevitably become exaggerated. This story, partly written soon after the time it occurred and then laid aside for the whole of the intervening period, does not suffer from this fault, though I must confess that, had I read it for the first time now, many years after the events it describes, I should have some difficulty in believing it. I must ask the reader to understand that I have attempted to tell the absolute truth.

* * *

---

[1] *Diet, Sanitation and Deficiency Disease*, DPH Dissertation, London School of Hygiene and Tropical medicine 1947.

Before we started from Surabaya, we were examined by a Japanese medical officer by being made to walk in single file past him. I am not aware that any man was rejected, those who could walk being deemed fit. We had a foretaste of things to come when we paraded in the camp on the morning of embarkation. The Senior British Officer – an unenviable position if ever there was one – Squadron Leader Pitts, was suddenly and without warning subjected to the most brutal beating-up that any of us had so far seen. This was in front of his assembled men. He was beaten about the head, ears and face and several times knocked to the ground, but he stood up to it well. It went on for fully 15 minutes and he finished up badly bruised and with at least one shattered eardrum. His assailant, a sergeant called Mori, was clearly impressing the whole company of rather over 2,000 mixed British and Dutch that he was in charge and prepared to get his own way by physical violence. We had seen such exhibitions before, less brutal, but they had always been the result of some real or imagined offence: this was entirely without warning or cause.

We had many occasions afterwards to witness – and experience – Mori's sadistic temperament, but what we had not realised at this time was that the brutalities of the individual Japanese increased, the further away he was from his headquarters. This was something we were to learn a good deal about. The brutalities meted out by the Nazis in Europe were politically organised; those of the Japanese were left to the individual soldier. Only one good point can be made: the more beastly the Japanese became, the more closely our men stood together. The experiences we were to have (though, clearly, we were no exceptions; the fate of those working on the Burma–Thailand Railway was quite as bad) involved probably the greatest degradation that Europeans have suffered in this century, with the exception of those unfortunates herded together in German concentration camps. But we had an advantage over them: we never, for long, lost two things – our sense of corporate discipline and our sense of humour. We also despised our captors. In many of our men, this brought out the very best; they became more unselfish, more helpful and more cooperative than ever I had known before and were capable of showing the greatest compassion.

We set out from Surabaya harbour for our unknown destination on 17 April 1943, having spent several days in the ships before we got under way. We were confined to the holds, where each man had just enough room to lie down, though touching those on each side of him and those at his head and feet. Even when we were being packed in in this way by Japanese soldiers with sticks, a sense of humour did not desert us, and many a man could not resist the temptation to shout 'baa', for the scene was indeed very reminiscent of sheep being driven into a lorry at a country market. Ventilation was totally inadequate for the tropical climate, though the holds were open, the only extra provision being a canvas tube leading down to the level where we lay, but with no air movement in it while we were stationary.

Sanitary facilities were primitive in the extreme – a platform with holes in it suspended from the side of the ship over the sea, to which one or two men could go at a time, having to climb over their mates to get there. It was immediately evident that we had brought a dysentery outbreak with us and the conditions were such, with no washing facilities, that an epidemic was inevitable. About 20 men with the disease were removed from the ship while we lay at anchor.

The number that finally set sail was 2,075. The days we waited in Surabaya harbour were quite dreadful – several hundred men in each hold of the ship in the tropics, a dysentery epidemic hovering, totally inadequate sanitary facilities and, until we moved, precious little ventilation. There was little to raise the spirits of the men, and altogether there was an air of deep depression. (I write as their doctor but think I have made it clear that we were all in the same situation.) Finally, we started moving and were at sea until 5 May, having covered the 1,200 miles to an island called Haruku. There was no marking on the side of the ship to indicate that prisoners of war were being carried.

Haruku is one of the Molucca group of islands – the Spice Islands – small coral islands of breathtaking beauty raised out of the sea by volcanic action. Our mission was to flatten the top of this island to make an air landing strip, presumably to facilitate the Japanese conquest of Australia.

It still astonishes me, many of my memories of that time being so clear, that I do not remember more about the details of this journey. The senses must have been numbed. The total absence of washing facilities and the difficulty – almost the impossibility – of handling a dysentery epidemic in the over-crowded hold of a ship were bad enough, but our life was made no easier at that time by the fact that the men, drawn from the large number at the Surabaya camp, had only recently come together, did not know each other well and were not yet any sort of unit. Many were separated from their friends and had not yet made new friendships (a matter of extreme significance in such a situation, straightforward friendship becoming of paramount importance in the struggle to survive). Perhaps most unsettling of all, we were off into the unknown with only one thing certain – it was going to be very unpleasant. There was, nevertheless, a remarkable absence of complaint; complaining was useless. When British troops touch rock bottom, it seems that they do what they can to alleviate the situation and they cuss, but then they grow philo-sophical; it struck me that this was a natural characteristic.

Nobody died on the journey though many were seriously ill on arrival.

* * *

Even though the details of the 18-day journey have rather receded in my memory, the next part of the story is vividly clear. We arrived at Haruku in torrential rain, rain that was to continue for many days. The camp site, in a nutmeg grove, had been cleared by native labour and the bamboo frames of *atap* huts erected. About half the huts had thatched palm roofs; the rest had none. The rain pelted down. The sanitary arrangements on our arrival were inadequate in the extreme: pits 3 feet deep, 2 feet wide and 12 feet long had been dug – and had been extensively used by the builders of the camp so that all of them were surging with a flowing mass of fly maggots. Because of the torrential rain, it did not take long for the pits to overflow with water, and within a day, streams of fly maggots were flowing away from them into the living-quarters (we were on sloping ground). Dysentery is spread by contamination of the food, or by contaminated material getting into the mouth by some other means, so it is not hard to see that, with a dysentery epidemic on our hands, the dissemination of infected material that was taking place all round us was potentially lethal.

Washing facilities existed, but in a river some 300 yards away with two or even three Japanese sentries to be passed and saluted each time one went there – always with the risk that some imagined (or real) insult would lead to a display of temper. This did not exactly encourage the men, almost dropping with fatigue, to wash, yet the only way to be sure of not catching dysentery was to wash before eating and before touching the mouth in any way – a counsel of perfection it was almost impossible for the men to observe. Flies – large bluebottles originating in the latrines – abounded and conveyed infection to any uncovered food, but there were more subtle ways in which infection could be spread. We had been issued with rubber-soled lace-up canvas boots at the start of our journey and clearly these became heavily contaminated with infection simply when we walked about the camp among the flowing maggots. Tying his bootlaces, therefore, became a means by which a man could become infected if, as was almost certain, he touched his mouth at some time after he put on his boots. It was quite impossible to expect the men to wash their hands each time they tied their bootlaces. Also, there was a little Javanese tobacco about the camp – and sufficient prayer-books to provide cigarette-paper. Few of the men, until they were told, realised that the very act of rolling a cigarette and putting it in the mouth after tying up the boot-laces was sufficient to give them dysentery.

This must be seen against a background of extreme over-crowding. Only half the huts had roofs, few had walls and the men were forced to go out to work on the runway immediately. As the native labour had been withdrawn, completion of the huts was very slow. All slept on the floor, which was damp with continuous rain, trying to avoid the rivulets that ran through almost every hut down the slope to the sea. There was only about enough room for every man to lie down and, in addition, many had lost their belongings on the journey. Their possessions did not amount to much, but each man had at least started with a blanket, the loss of which was serious. All in all, our plight was such that many were simply too tired or too dispirited to care whether they caught dysentery or not. Death in a short while seemed so utterly inevitable that I am sure, at that time, many would not have minded whether it came soon or late. And the rain teemed down. But the depression was only a temporary phase; we did not realise it at the time, but it appeared to be part of Japanese policy to try to break our spirit by disorganising us. It failed hopelessly, because each time they tried it we were driven closer together.

We, the medical staff, had to try to cope with the dysentery epidemic as well as doing what we could to prevent new cases occurring, which was very little. We arrived with about 100 cases; the infection spread like wildfire through the camp, and, before long, more than half the men were down. There were several doctors, both Dutch and British. Alastair Forbes – from whom I had parted at Tasik Malaja – and myself were the British representatives. Clifford Beales, a dental surgeon, was with us too, and there was a skilled Dutch pharmacist. A second British dentist came, but insisted on being in charge of the cookhouse and did no dentistry. At the height of the epidemic, with 1,100 men ill, only two of the doctors (of whom I was one) were on their feet.

We tried to make urgent representations to the Japanese Commandant – the Japanese having insisted upon being in total charge of camp organization – to make an immediate improvement in the sanitary situation. Clearly, we had to scrap the existing shallow trench latrines at once. As the greatest menace was the flies, even after the acute present danger from the surging maggots had subsided as the rain stopped, some means had to be devised to stop them breeding. (At

41

Semarang, I had done this by keeping the contents of the pit so alkaline with quicklime that they could not breed, but that was a smaller problem and, anyway, we had no quicklime at Haruku.) The choices open to us in ordinary circumstances would have been to make the latrines flyproof with wooden baffles – impossible as the only wood available was bamboo; to make deep boreholes – impossible as we had no auger; or to erect a platform over the sea – eminently possible as we were beside the seashore. This last solution would, we considered, immediately remove all the danger.

There was a Japanese interpreter – Cassiama – who figures largely in this story, and we finally obtained an interview. I did not know the name of the Commandant, (a lieutenant), though we called him Arthur Askey because of a slight imagined resemblance to that delightful gentleman. He spent his time hitting out at imaginary enemies with a wooden imaginary sword; it must have been very difficult for him to know – as the whole thing was make-believe – whether he was doing it well or badly. We went before him, bowed to the necessary 15 degrees at the waist while saluting, and told him of our problems. He listened to the interpreted statement as if he had not up to that time realised that there was any problem. We told him of the danger to his own guards if he took no action; we told him of the only possible solution – a platform latrine over the sea. He dismissed us, saying that he would give us his answer later. We bowed to 15 degrees, saluted and departed.

Two days later, we were summoned to the presence again. We were told that the Japanese regarded the sanitary arrangements as entirely satisfactory and that it was impossible to make a latrine over the sea. The reason for this, he said, was simple. The sea belonged to His Imperial Highness the Nipponese Emperor (breath was always drawn in sharply through closed teeth after mentioning His Highness) and nobody was to do that sort of thing in the Emperor's property. He told us that he had the answer to our troubles. Each man was to catch a hundred flies a day. 'A hundred fries, mind,' shouted Cassiama, and we were dismissed. The Japanese insisted on this fly-catching exercise and inspected the catches for a period of months after this. How much extra dysentery was caused by the men having to handle infected flies in this manner, we shall never know. The fly population, certainly, appeared totally unaffected.

All men who could stand had to go to work on the airstrip, and all the time the dysentery epidemic raged. It was of the type caused by the organism known as *Flexner* and was not the most serious variety, so the men, not yet feeling the full effects of dietary deficiency, did not die in the acute stage of the illness; but many did later, when the combination of the after-effects of the disease and the gross deficiencies in their diet overcame them. This pattern was to change as time went on, when men already debilitated by privation fell victims. They died in the acute stage.

May and June 1943 were a nightmare. We had precious little in the way of medicines to treat the men. We had some magnesium sulphate (Epsom salts) and a little of a flavine derivative called Rivanol in the form of pills. Apart from this, we had to rely on natural remedies, helped by our able Dutch pharmacist. A native remedy, a bark called *gambir* which contained tannin, was given as a powder and was most useful in mild cases. If we required a purgative, and in those days before modern drugs, purgatives had a place in the treatment, we either drew on our meagre supply of Epsom salts or we used sea water diluted 50 per cent with rainwater. Many vomited after it, but if retained, it sometimes had a purgative effect. For those who, because of the severity of their illness, became dehydrated, we made up a solution of salt in boiled water – a so-called isotonic solution (we had a chemist's balance to weigh quantities) – and gave it under the skin, using one of our minute stock of needles. It always caused a slight feverish reaction but this seemed to do no harm – indeed, many seemed rather to enjoy the shiver it gave them; it made a change. ('Oh! It's lovely, Doc. It gives me a cheap thrill'). The fortitude of our patients, knowing they were near death, was impressive to see and share.

The epidemic continued in July but finally the ferocity of it died down in August. By scrupulous attention to detail, by

43

collecting rainwater from the roof to wash in, by giving thought to every movement which might bring infection to my mouth – by almost adopting an operating-theatre technique to eating – I avoided infection even though continuously in contact with it which was fortunate, because never were medical personnel so necessary as in those dismal days – but my turn was to come later.

As the epidemic died down, an equally serious problem arose which clearly we expected, but could do little to alleviate. Almost without exception, those who had had dysentery started to show signs of vitamin deficiency disease; but before I go into this, something should be said about the food we were given.

The staple food was rice, polished white rice, which, if eaten without sufficient meat and vegetables, inevitably leads to vitamin deficiency disease. The amount of meat and vegetables received was never sufficient, and although, with the various means we devised to supplement the rations, those who managed to avoid infection remained relatively healthy though grossly wasted, even a mild attack of dysentery would send a man into severe deficiency. And those who had had dysentery seriously were nearly all doomed. The vitamins we lacked were those known as the B complex, notably, in the terminology of that time, vitamins B 1 and B 2 (the names I shall use throughout this account[2]). Lack of these vitamins causes, respectively, diseases known as beriberi and pellagra.

The Japanese ration for a fit man was:

Rice (weighed uncooked)	400–600 grams daily
Green vegetables	10–30 grams daily
Meat	30 grams weekly
Some sugar, salt and oil	

---

[2]The vitamin B complex is a group of many substances necessary for health. The three that concern us here are thiamin (then called vitamin B 1), riboflavine and niacin (then grouped together as vitamin B 2). Niacin is sometimes called nicotinic acid. These three substances are particularly necessary when the diet is predominantly carbohydrate, as ours was.

ERRATUM

Page 125, line 17 :
'villains of the peace' should read 'villains of the piece'

For a sick man on light work, the rice ration was dropped from 400 to 250 grams daily and hospital patients had 150 grams. These quantities were, so far as we could tell, decided by Sergeant Mori, the idea of the graduated ration being, we were told, to encourage the sick men to get up and work. In fact, as we found that sacks of rice destined for us were being sold to the native population of the island, he clearly had a vested interest in keeping the diet of the sick at starvation level. The rice was filthy, some of it evidently dockside sweepings, and often needed picking over by hand before it was cooked. A fair amount of polishings remained in it and we tried to encourage the cooks not to wash this out as it contained some of the vitamin B complex that had been ground off during polishing. When we tried to impress upon the Japanese that we were suffering from vitamin B deficiency disease and that many were dying from it, they gave us halibut oil capsules, rich in vitamin D, the one we already had an excess of as we were working in tropical sunshine. These capsules nevertheless had a slight advantage; they tasted fishy, and even that flavour, nauseating in ordinary circumstances, was better than no flavour, so we ate them with our rice.

The vegetables were mainly the leaves of the tapioca plant, so hard and indigestible that many failed to retain them. They were bitter and we used part of our small sugar ration to try to make them more palatable. The meat, one ounce weekly, was dried water-buffalo, occasionally supplemented by dog, killed as I have already described. Dog is quite good to eat, but it helps not to know it is dog. Surprisingly, the small amount of meat was the aspect of our diet that worried us least, but the flavour of it, even though the water-buffalo meat stank to high heaven, was very welcome. Clearly, our protein intake was far below a healthy level because we saw many patients with swelling of the legs evidently due to protein deficiency.

We supplemented our diet, by fair means and foul. In fact, we picked, caught or stole anything that appeared edible. The surprising thing is that so few were made ill by eating poisonous plants. A few days after we arrived at our camp on

45

Haruku there was hardly a green leaf left – all had been picked and eaten. We found, in common with all who have tried before, that grass has no nutritive value to the human race unless first processed by a herbivorous animal. Only one case of plant poisoning occurred to my knowledge and that was from eating the bulbs of a lily-like plant. The four or five men who did this were badly upset for a few days but recovered. Various sources of protein occasionally walked about the camp, in particular, tortoises and iguanas. Tortoises were good to eat but I found it most difficult to kill them before boiling. Trying to decapitate a tortoise with a knife is almost impossible – the only thing that it can do fast is to retract its head. To boil them to death, as is done with lobsters, revolted me, even in those circumstances, and they have such accusing eyes. But one did it. Iguanas – large, rather slow, tree-climbing lizards – make a very good stew, hardly distinguishable from chicken, but one required either luck or skill with a catapult to catch them. Alligator tasted foul, however hungry one was, and python was tough, as were parrots. Once, in honour of some Japanese feast, late at night, in total darkness, we were all given cooked fish. Mine was in two pieces, so I ate one at once and saved the other for the morning. I noticed an unusual flavour, but fried fish, even cold, was a luxury not to be lightly declined. The piece I saved, I brought out for breakfast – and immediately discovered the cause of the unusual flavour: it was crawling with well-developed fly-maggots. But I came to no harm as a result of this.

We were beside the seashore; there were fish in the sea, but nobody had either time or fish-hooks to catch them, and anyone fit enough to catch fish had to do outside work on the airstrip. occasionally, on some Japanese feast-day, when we were given a half holiday, some of the prisoners would go to the water's edge and catch shoals of fish-fry in their mosquito nets – a practice we had warned them against, as an intact mosquito net was a life-saving piece of equipment, even though there was no malaria at Haruku. We never knew if our next port of call would be malarial: in fact, it was, but by then so many had died that there were enough nets to go round, even though some had been spoiled by fishing.

Obviously, to cultivate vegetables would have greatly alleviated our troubles, but gardening at this time was impossible. So many were ill with dysentery that the Japanese insisted that every man who could stand was to work on the airstrip, so there was nobody who could have tended gardens.

This, then, was the ration position in the early days of the dysentery epidemic. There was a camp shop which stocked food, of which I shall tell more later, but it did nothing to help the diet of the sick. I shall return to the whole question of what we ate but have made this digression to put the matter of vitamin deficiency into perspective. In short, our rations were insufficient to keep a fit man much above starvation level, and for a man recently ill with an infection, they were tragically inadequate.

Somehow, in our first few weeks at Haruku, we managed to complete the buildings of the camp, at least in so far as every man had a sleeping place off the ground in a hut, and we had a hospital – two *atap* huts, each holding about 80 patients, and both were full. We were at a time now – in June – when the earlier patients with dysentery were recovering from the acute infection and, in many instances, slipping into deficiency disease, while new cases were still occurring, though not so frequently as before. Life was busy for the medical staff. I well remember, after doing a round of my 80 patients each morning, coming out in a cold sweat and having to sit down before the time of the mid-day meal (breakfast having been rice gruel) because standing was no longer possible. The condition was similar to that of a diabetic who has had too much insulin and was almost certainly due to hypoglycaemia (a dangerous lowering of the blood-sugar level), so near were we to starvation. I still wonder whether, apart from, I hope, a valuable psychological boost, our efforts as doctors did very much to alter the course of the illness. Certainly, those who were seriously ill nearly all died, often with immense fortitude, even good humour, and after a pitiable struggle. We saw conditions which the medical textbooks of my student days said no longer existed, in particular, *Cancrum oris* where, in the space

47

of a few days, the cheeks and mouth rot away, leaving the lower half of the face a large, foul cavity, the patient dying in appalling agony. This was made indescribably worse by the hordes of bluebottles that came on the rotting surfaces to lay their eggs, with results that are better left to the imagination.

Those who had a milder attack of dysentery and recovered from it, only to become the victims of deficiency disease, now became our main concern. Far and away the commonest manifestation, so common that few in the camp were spared, was the condition well-named 'happy feet' by the men. It was a burning sensation in the soles of the feet, felt when at rest, particularly at night. Some relief was obtained by getting up and walking about, so many suffered serious loss of sleep. Every night there would be several men walking, even dancing, outside their huts, trying to get relief. The cause of it was a neuritis affecting the nerves of the legs, and it often advanced to shooting pains involving not only the feet but the legs and thighs as well. It was due to a lack of vitamin B 1, and though it affected most, those who had had dysentery and been spared, myself included, were also victims. Along with this, there was a sore tongue and mouth and much skin trouble, due to a shortage of vitamin B 2, the condition known as pellagra. This, at least, we could cure later on: it so happens that the small, extremely fiery chillie which grows easily in Indonesia and is known as the lombok is very rich in vitamin B 2. If men with sore mouths can eat these chillies – an almost unbearable thing to do – they can be cured. And the men did.

One of the most serious forms of neuritis due to vitamin B 1 deficiency affected the optic nerve and therefore the eyesight. Books were in short supply, but there were some, and frequently the first complaint from a patient was that he had started reading a book and had suddenly, so suddenly that he knew at which line on which page he first noticed it, found that the print was 'dancing' and he had difficulty in making his eyes pass from one line to the next. Characteristically, he said that when he looked at a line of print, some of the words were missing, and if the condition was more advanced, when he looked at people's bodies, he could not see their heads. It soon appeared that the condition was irreversible, so it was extremely serious. We were able later to take measures to supplement our diet with yeast and so prevent the onset of further cases, but no amount of yeast would cure those already affected.

Some who had had severe dysentery went into a state of heart failure from acute beriberi before they died, but just a few managed to survive the heart failure, and one, to my knowledge, lived until we left Haruku, and I think until his final release.

The task of the Haruku camp was to flatten the top of the volcanic island to make an airstrip, and the hard fact of it was that, as we were a working camp, sickness was not taken into account; all men were to work. Obviously, this was impossible; many of the men were ill, and at one time more than half were far too ill to work. So there was a continual bone of contention between the Japanese and ourselves, particularly between the Japanese and the medical staff, who were quite clear in their minds that they had a duty to prevent the Japanese exploiting sick men. Each evening, in this dismal period between May and August 1943, the Japanese interpreter, Cassiama, would appear at the camp office telling us how many men were required for outside work the following day, and each morning the battle would begin. A certain number of men were obviously sufficiently fit, and conversely a number too sick for there to be any question of them working. In between were a few dozen who were unfit for work by our standards but from whose numbers the working party must be made up. If we, the medical staff, stood firm and refused to let these men go out, then we soon learned from bitter experience that the Japanese would go through the hospital with sticks and beat up any man they thought fit to go out – and generally try to intimidate the sick. At one time this was an almost daily occurrence. If this method failed, and inevitably it always did, then Mori would cut the rations to the hospital patients to below starvation level in an effort to make the men discharge themselves. So we were forced to make a compromise, letting men, quite unfit by our standards, go to work in order to have a chance to let those in hospital recover – or die in peace. We understood this, the men in the middle group, unfit for work but available, understood it, and they were magnificent. Many mornings there was a beating-up at the work parades, and always there was great unpleasantness. Alastair Forbes, who throughout this time did the British out-patient clinics, had the unenviable daily task of trying to force the hand of the Japanese, and did it splendidly.

The Dutch, of course, suffered in exactly the same way. The two groups ran separate out-patient clinics, chiefly because of language problems, and one of the Dutch medical officers attended the parades and argued for his men alongside Forbes. The one thing we had to prevent at all costs was to lose all control over the handling of the sick, and because of the efforts of these two doctors, the situation, though dreadful, was not quite so bad as it otherwise might have been.

The reduction in the hospital ration, to make men discharge themselves, was far from an idle threat. As soon as the huts which served as wards became full, the ration would be cut. This usually meant that each man received half his normal rice ration in the form of gruel or 'pap' and no vegetables at all. Whereas, when such restrictions were not in force, we ignored the different scales of ration for sick and well men, giving everybody the same share, when the hospital ration was cut, the Japanese supervised distribution and each man had literally three mugs of gruel a day. This might continue for two or three weeks and always resulted in an explosion of fresh cases of vitamin deficiency disease and eventually in many more deaths, not only from deficiency disease but also from sheer starvation. On not less than five occasions did this happen, and it was an act of diabolical cruelty on the part of the Japanese. The rows of men in the hospital, skeletons clothed in a thin layer of muscle and skin, is a sight I shall not forget. The picture was the same as was seen all too frequently in German concentration camps at the end of the war in Europe. What impressed me most was that our chaps managed to stay cheerful and courteous to each other. They were ordinary men, and once again, one was made to feel rather humble, seeing the quality of the human spirit – with certain death only a few days away.

The purpose of the ration cut was twofold – apart from any profit on the side the Japanese made from selling rice. First, Mori thought it an effective way of making anyone who was malingering discharge himself, and second, perhaps more important, it was an attempt to force the hand of the medical staff to discharge patients so that larger working parties would be available. All protests to the Japanese were met with the same reply: there were too many in hospital, which meant that we were bad doctors. To quote Cassiama: 'We give you a beautiful hospital and what do you do? You fill it up. You are bad doctors.' It was made clear to us that once the number in hospital was reduced, the ration would be restored. Unfortunately, the measure was bound to be effective. it was better to discharge the less ill, so that all did not succumb to deficiency disease or starvation; but those who were discharged did little to swell the number of the working party, except on paper. Also, when a hospital ration cut was in force, fewer men reported sick, the majority preferring to carry on working even though ill, rather than go into hospital to face possible death from starvation. This reduction in the out-patient clinics was held by the Japanese to justify their claim that many of the men in hospital were malingering, and they mocked us.

Another trick tried by the Japanese to make the men discharge themselves from hospital was very simple. They ordered all the doctors, to go out of the camp on roadbuilding, their reasoning being that with no medical care, the patients would get up and walk out. It did not work, the vast majority of the men were far too ill.

* * *

It was many weeks of slogging work, coping with the dysentery epidemic, before we could really look around us and take stock of our situation. The island of Haruku is, as I said, a coral island brought above sea level – indeed, turned into a small mountain – by volcanic action. It is beautiful, fertile and

51

renowned throughout the world for its butterflies. The other islands in the Moluccas group are Ceram, Buru, Ambon and Saparua, all covered by lush vegetation and separated by narrow seas whose astonishingly clear blue colour has to be seen to be believed. The industry of Haruku before our coming, or rather, before the few Europeans left, was the production of spices – nutmeg, mace (which is found within the shell of the nutmeg, a red fibrous material) and probably chillies, which grow easily in the rich soil. Our camp occupied a nutmeg plantation, through which the dusty road led down to a wooden jetty extending about a hundred yards on to the coral reef which surrounded our part of the island. The camp entrance was flanked by two ancient masonry posts, and just within, beside the road, was an object that made us proud – a steamroller with 'Foden Ltd. Kent, England' emblazoned on a brass plate at the front. It was apparently in perfect condition, parked there by its last owners, probably having been brought to the island to help improve the roads. To see this example of British engineering craftsmanship gave us no end of pleasure. I shall return to this steamroller later.

The native people we saw lived in a village close behind the camp and had clearly had some contact with European missionaries, because they could sometimes be heard singing well-known hymn-tunes, the words of which I could never discern. This was particularly impressive when we heard them at dead of night, out in their boats, fishing. They rowed, and presumably to keep time in the darkness, sang hymn-tunes, beating out the rhythm with their paddles on the side of the boat.

Ironically, food was far from scarce on Haruku island. So many were the fish in the sea and so fertile the ground that the locals managed to keep comfortably well-fed on what appeared to me to be about two days' work a week, fishing at night, or using round throwing-nets by day, and doing a little gardening. The fish they caught were partly eaten fresh, but many were dried in the hot sun and some, from their flavour, were kippered, presumably over smouldering bamboo chips. Their gardens grew sweet potatoes, tapioca, tomatoes, bananas, chillies, citronella grass and, I have no doubt, other crops. The tapioca, they grew for the roots; I am sure they did not eat the leaves as we had to, and properly prepared, tapioca root can be palatable and useful. The dreadful custom of serving it as a glutinous mass – the only way we know in this country – was probably quite unknown to the local people of Haruku. It made, with a little water and coconut oil, a passable pastry, as I learned later to my advantage when I had to manage on frog pies.

Food was also up the trees. Coconuts abounded and only required somebody with a head for heights and the skill to climb the tree and knock them down. The trees in the camp were very soon cleared of their nuts, so we had no lasting advantage from this, but I still remember, in the early days, being given a recently fallen green coconut with the end hacked off with a *parang* (a formidable heavy knife) and drinking the slightly effervescent water (so-called milk) from it. No champagne ever tasted so good. It ran down your face and down your shirt as well. Papayas also grew abundantly on low trees. They are a soft melon-like fruit which could have been a useful supplement to our rations, but the Japanese always picked them as soon as they were ripe. The only thing for us to do was to pick those that we could grow while they were still unripe and use them as vegetables. This was very hard on the hands of those who had to cut up and prepare them as they contain a powerful digestive ferment (papain) now used in western medicine, but then a great nuisance. When we first arrived, bananas grew in the camp, but we soon ate them all, and it was useless to try to grow our own as the Japanese took them.

The Japanese occasionally went fishing on the reef just beyond the shore. They used dynamite, one explosion bringing up dozens of fish. They sometimes gave us a few, but this was rare.

* * *

That we should be dying of starvation among all this plenty simply highlighted our tragic situation, but it also indicated that Mori was no fool. He knew that starvation was his most powerful weapon. The whole Japanese attitude, in any case, indicated to me that we were being allowed to survive only because – and probably as long as – it was in their interest that we did so. If starving us was, in their view, the way to keep us in submission – and working – then we were starved. Also, they remained to some extent afraid of us, or that was my impression, and they dared not allow us to become too well-fed and possibly dangerous. We were, after all, many miles from any sizeable Japanese garrison.

From what I have already said, it is probably quite clear that Mori, the NCO, ran the camp. The officer nominally in charge seemed neither to know nor care what went on. ('Askey' had, I think, left and 'the Goat', a major so-called because of his foot-long straggly beard, had come. Like Askey, he spent his time hitting out at imaginary enemies with a wooden imaginary sword, but he had a slightly improved technique: he shouted while he did it.) Mori was responsible for arranging the working party, beating the prisoners, closing the hospital and generally making our lives a misery, ably abetted by Cassiama, the interpreter, who knew which side his bread was buttered. He was an ordinary soldier, and if in Mori's good books could expect a happy life. Between them, they had absolute power over our fate.,

Cassiama boasted that he was taught English by Mrs Johnson, a missionary in Tokyo. He certainly had a sufficient command of it to be a thorn in our flesh, not only acting as interpreter for Mori but hanging around in corners so that he could report back to his master what we were talking about. The good Mrs Johnson had a great deal to answer for. Usually, somebody spotted him when he was listening in to us, and whoever saw him gave a warning that was understood by all of us but was rather too subtle for Cassiama himself – he whistled the first two bars of *A Tisket, a Tasket*, a song popular before the war. The next line is 'A little yellow basket'. Whenever we complained about the treatment of the sick and tried to convince the Japanese that many men were not only very ill but dying, his cry was always the same: 'You

54

lie, you lie.' One was reminded very forcefully of the predicament of the Children of Israel as reported in the fifth chapter of Exodus. They were also, in a sense, prisoners of a totalitarian power, on working parties for their captors, and one felt for them. Between the two of them, Mori and Cassiama had so much power – and apparently so little supervision – that it would have been surprising had they not made what they could on the side by fiddling our rations.

The other guards, Japanese-trained Koreans, were insignificant. To us, they had no separate identity. They marched exceedingly sloppily about the camp, guarded all the paths, required to be saluted whenever a prisoner, officer or other rank, passed them, and required to be told if one was going to the lavatory, the Japanese for which, phonetically, was *Banjo ni ikki mass*, one of the few phrases everyone knew, apart from the numbers and the orders used on parade.

I have been asked at times why we did not try to escape. Clearly, this was out of the question for a medical officer, but anyway escape was impracticable. The native population were far too frightened of the Japanese ever to try to conceal a prisoner and, as I have mentioned, had little incentive to do so – we were not allies in the accepted sense of the word. Also, we had no access to boats on our part of the island – and most important, nowhere to go. Several attempts were made by prisoners to escape from other camps, all unsuccessful and all punished by death, by shooting in the early days and latterly by bayoneting, the victim having first to dig his own grave. This contrasts strongly with the light-hearted pranks of prisoners in the German camps, where escaping was looked on as a game – and was rarely punished by death. It was clear to everyone that there was only one way out of the camp and that was in a coffin.

A very strange medical fact emerged: even though we were living in the most deplorable and, if one thought too much, apparently hopeless conditions, nobody ever came to me with anything remotely approaching what is called a nervous breakdown. This was a very different story from the days of the fall of Singapore when escape was possible by ship.

55

Men died at the rate of approximately 90 each month in these early days at Haruku. We tried to make them some sort of coffin from split bamboo, at least at first, but later this material became scarce and we could no longer provide coffins. We buried our dead with a simple service in a small green plateau at the edge of the shore a hundred yards or so from the camp boundary. Their personal friends – or such of them as could stand – were there. The graves were only shallow; the men did not have the strength to dig deep. The certification of these deaths presented no problem to the Japanese: at the beginning of each month an adequate number of death certificates was sent to us with the demand that they be signed. They were otherwise blank. They were then returned to the Japanese to fill in as necessary and used to cover the deaths of the coming month. The Japanese never left us in any doubt that we either obeyed them or they killed us, so we simply had to acquiesce in this juggling with medical ethics.

Surprisingly as it may seem, as the Japanese fulfilled no other provision of the Geneva Convention, they went through the motions of paying us for our services. The men on the outside working party were paid 15 cents (approximately 4p) for a day's work. I was paid 125 dollars (or guilders, depending on where I was) a month,[3] for which I had to 'sign' with my thumbprint in red ink. The currency with which we were paid was paper money, the notes unnumbered, but stating that the Japanese Bank promised to pay the bearer one dollar (or guilder). The Japanese printed this money in vast quantities – and in some parts, particularly Singapore, the Chinese printed it even faster. Of my 125 dollars, 120 were retained by the Japanese to put into the Japanese Bank, leaving me with 5. Of this, the major part, sometimes as much as 4 dollars 50 cents, was retained to be put into the 'camp fund' which existed to buy our vegetable ration, we were told, from the native population of Haruku. As our vegetable ration was supplied by the Japanese anyway, it is clear that the camp fund went into

---

[3]Approximately £14 at that time.

56

Mori's pocket. So my spending money was something between 50 cents and a couple of dollars per month. I was a poor relation compared with those strong enough to work on the outside party, earning 15 cents a day, but they supported their friends.

The camp shop, run by Mori, was the place where the money could be spent. The stock was extremely variable, but there were sometimes kippered local fish – which were very good. Coconuts, from which the oil could be easily extracted, sugar and chillies were also sometimes available. But the shop was tied up with a subtle system of blackmail. Before any purchase could be made, you had to have a 'shop ticket', which was a slip of paper given out automatically to the outside working party for one day's work, but for everybody else the issue of tickets depended entirely upon Mori's whim. This system meant that the walking sick, those on light camp duties and, of course, the hospital patients themselves – those who most needed the small supplements that the shop would provide – had neither pay nor tickets. Everything militated against the recovery of the sick. Everything Mori did made it clear that the choice was to be outside work or starvation, with sickness not taken into account.

Obviously, private sharing among friends was universal. The most firm loyalties developed among groups of men, each group carrying their mates when they fell sick. Such was their fierce devotion to each other that few would have hesitated to give their lives for their friends, and in a subtle way, many did. Often, they shared their rations to the extent that they themselves fell ill. The doctors often had a thin time when it came to shop tickets: Mori sometimes withheld them from us for a month if he considered too many men were in hospital, but if he was not feeling very well himself, they were lavished upon us. Especially was this so when he was expecting to have a minor operation. When we were really low, the men, if they could, looked after us, bringing us a share of what they had managed to steal, but more of that later.

By September, 370 of our company had died and the Japanese suddenly informed us that they had decided to remove

57

the sick men from the camp. 'Sick' was a relative term, but at least it gave us the chance to send back to Java those men for whom we saw no hope of recovery under the conditions at Haruku. In all, 650 went, leaving just over 1,000 behind. The party travelled in relays from the jetty on a raft as the water was too shallow for the ships to come alongside. On one of these journeys, the raft capsized, tossing everybody into the water. Among us, watching them go, was a Dutchman, who said quietly, '*Partir, c'est mourir un peu*' – all culture was not lost. They were all pulled out and reached the ship minus what small personal belongings they had had, but the Dutchman's words were rather too near the truth. several hundred of them were lost when their ship was sunk by Allied action. (see p. 101). Such ships were unmarked; there was no indication that their holds were filled with Allied prisoners. Among the men remaining at Haruku were 20 whom we considered too ill to survive the journey.

Pictures of Haruku, saved from discovery by being hidden between the layers of my pack

HARUKU CAMP

HARUKU CAMP

Above: The three Japanese, who were mainly responsible for our brutally harsh treatment and high death rate, at the time of their trial

Right: The kingfisher carved in teak (so called 'bastard teak' used as fuel for the railways in Java)

4

HARUKU II. YEAST

As soon as the party of sick had left for Java, two of the medical staff were ordered to go and see the Japanese Commandant. We were told that, as a result of a piece of Japanese inspiration, a latrine must be built over the sea. We were given quite a lecture on the skill of Japanese Army engineers in these matters. I do not know whether the officer whom we knew as 'the Goat' was even aware that we had put the idea forward to his predecessor on our arrival several months before or whether, more likely, they were saving face for themselves (a matter of utmost importance to the Japanese). The essential thing was that at last, far too late, we should have control of the public health position with regard to dysentery.

The structure was soon made out of bamboo and *atap*; it had a superb view across coral sea to the wooded island of Ceram, and though our health problems were far from over, acute bacillary dysentery ceased to be one of them. The new latrine was a pleasant place to visit, though sharks occasionally swam alarmingly close beneath. It was simply a bamboo platform with a series of holes along its length and no privacy at all, but this had one advantage – a little small-talk could be exchanged between the occupants. My next-door neighbour, squatting beside me, summed it up very well one day when he said: 'You know, Doc, this is the only real bit of pleasure that's left in life.'

This part of the shore became very heavily populated with crabs. They were easy to catch but, regrettably, had a characteristic flavour and obviously required thorough cooking.

Few people tried them more than once, which is probably just as well as they could have been a serious source of danger from infection.

The medical staff, Dutch and British, lived together at the end of the hut occupied by officers. The three British members, Alastair Forbes, Clifford Beales, the dentist, and I slept in a row. Forbes, as I have said, ran the British out-patient clinics and had the difficult task of haggling daily with the Japanese, who were trying to force the sick out to work. Such a rapport did he have with his men that on many occasions someone really quite unfit would go out so that others could stay back – this was the prevailing spirit among the vast majority. Nobody, however bad he felt, ever argued with Forbes' decisions. I looked after British in-patients, did what pathological investigation was possible and stood in for Forbes if for any reason he could not attend the work parade or look after the out-patients, as he did for me in the wards when necessary.

Clifford Beales looked after our teeth very effectively and was expected to do the same for the Japanese. He had an *atap* surgery, a few instruments and a treadle drill. One of his more worrying activities was removing the gold caps from the teeth of Japanese guards which had been put on by the Chinese when they were fighting in China. As I said earlier, the Japanese found this a convenient way of taking loot home, but the Chinese dentists, rather cleverly, put the cap over a carious tooth if there was one. By now, some of these were giving trouble and poor Cliff had the rather tricky task of taking the cap off without the tooth coming with it. He had his moments of anxiety but, so far as I know, he never failed, and his work did help us with shop tickets. It seems highly incongruous that though we were threatened all the time by starvation, we were able to receive expert dental treatment.

Of the Dutch doctors, one chiefly remembers – as all the British troops do with gratitude – Rudi Springer. An excellent surgeon, he would turn his hand to any medical task. He was a tower of philosophical strength when things went wrong, as they so often did, and he had a ready wit. He had the double burden, as did many of the Dutch, of knowing that his wife and two children were interned, but not where. They survived and we have all met since. None of the rank and file in that camp has ever forgotten Springer; he was so good to everybody, even those who annoyed him. He once said to me, of some British soldier, 'That man makes me so angry that I am very careful to give him the best treatment I can.' This sums up Springer: deeply conscientious, no matter what the circumstances.

On rare occasions, because of illness among the staff, I had to do the Dutch out-patient clinic. Many of the Dutch spoke excellent English, but obviously some did not. I understood Dutch well but spoke it only slowly, which made the sick parade rather laborious; but worse, all the names of anatomical parts that I knew, I had learned from the soldiery themselves, and when the words referred to the nether regions, they were not among the most polite. The sick parade was held in public, the queue of men waiting to be seen being in the same room. My attempts to obtain a history of whatever complaint the man had, using my coarse vocabulary, lent an air of gaiety, to say the least, to the proceedings. At times, the room fairly resounded with laughter – and I did not know which of my faltering words were the really impolite ones.

We did not have much time off, just the occasional afternoon when there was some Japanese public holiday. We had a few books, most of which were Chinese pirate editions of well-known Western works. One such was *The Water Gipsies* by Sir Alan Herbert. These pirate copies were not bound in the usual manner but were printed as separate pages which were then glued together along the spine, so eventually, in the tropics, the glue came apart and all the pages were again separate. Our copy of *The Water Gipsies* was in this state, and on one of these free afternoons we were all able to read the book at the same time, each man reading a page then handing it to his neighbour on the left. It was a valuable moment of relief in our time at Haruku. I had a copy of James Jeans' *The Expanding Universe*, a good book in such a situation, difficult, but just comprehensible to me; Gilbert White's *Natural*

History of Selbourne; and the Bible, which was a good standby because it was possible to read about people as badly off as ourselves and also – truth to tell – it made passable cigarette-paper.

We invented games to occupy the dark lampless evenings. There was, of course, no electricity; coconut oil was the only fuel, and it was wrong to burn what we could eat. One game with limitless possibilities was a general knowledge quiz about some area of London: 'If you stand with your back to the front door of the Palladium, what is in front of you, to the right, to the left?' – and so on. Perhaps not surprisingly, in our deprived condition, we always seemed in the end to get back to that delightful – and so innocent – place, The Windmill Theatre, with its naked young ladies, and Mrs Laura Henderson, its silver-haired founder, who cannot even remotely have suspected what she was founding when she thought of her non-stop variety theatre for out-of-work actors. Most evocative – even painfully so – these evenings could be.

There was little that Clifford Beales and I did not finally know about each other. We had food fantasies and invented meals. Strangely, they were not elaborate, just food: I required nothing more than a tin of corned beef, a tin-opener, a new loaf of crusty bread and some butter. The loaf was hollowed out, the inside buttered, the corned beef inserted uncut and the whole thing slowly eaten – a day-dream that lasted me for hours. The truth was that we were so hungry, and so chronic was our hunger, that it ceased to be hunger in the real sense of the word; it was simply a never-ending feeling of discomfort.

In these strange circumstances, many of us liked to have some special possession – something to take pride in. Some lavished quite disproportionate care upon their aluminium eating-dish, polishing it until it shone; others found themselves an old tin can and, with the help of a piece of wire, fashioned a handle and made a mug – and kept it shining like a mirror. Our only polishing materials were sand and toothpowder, of which, for some reason, we were provided with a large stock. For myself, I had my pair of trousers, bought at Esselmont and MacIntosh in Aberdeen. They became a sort of talisman, carefully patched where they wore through and pressed at night under my blanket. I also had my little kingfisher, carved from teak at Surabaya, and I am sure that the possession of these things had, in a strange way, a great survival value.

Rats abounded in our quarters, large rats. Some people ate them if they could catch them; I never did. They took articles of our clothing and built nests of them in the thatched roof. Clifford Beales once lost his leather belt and his underclothes, only to discover them later as part of a rat's nest. Any food we possessed had to be hung up as far out of their reach as possible.[1]

We catered, in so far as private catering was possible, in small groups of friends who shared each other's good luck and bad. If one of the group came by a shop ticket and there was some money, then all had a small piece of kipper that evening; if more than one of the group was lucky, then we might arrange a planned menu. The best way to use any scraps of food we could lay our hands on was to make a *nasigoreng*, the main basis of which was rice, and it could be very good. For this, you needed your ration of boiled rice, whatever scraps of fish or vegetables you could find, finely chopped, some salt and a little coconut oil. For luxury, you also needed chillies and onions and, most important – and most difficult to come by – some firewood, or a share in somebody else's fire. Our aluminium eating-dishes would do double duty as frying-pans or saucepans, and in fact the size of the group who could share together was to a great extent determined by the size of the cooking vessels they had.

To make a *nasigoreng*, your fish bits were first braised in coconut oil with your vegetables, onions and a chilli or two. When all was good and brown and, if possible, crisp – and smelled delightful – the rice ration was added and the whole cooked for a little longer to spread the oil through the rice. We soon learned that the fire of a chilli (for which the local

---

[1]It is reliably reported that they nibbled the toes of some sleeping prisoners. Leslie Audus, who figures considerably in this story later on, was one victim.

people use a special word – *pedis* – as opposed to the heat of a fire – *panas*) was inversely proportional to the size and subtly connected with the colour; really small green ones, which look so harmless, can be most painful when you are not used to them.

What a marvellous thing is the onion. We grew a few and managed to come by a few from the shop, and no experience has so convinced me of its inestimable worth. Any meal, however dull, can, if you are hungry (and by God, we were hungry!) be turned into a banquet with the help of some salt and an onion or two. Moreover, the smell of onions cooking can whet the appetite of everybody within 50 yards. The creation of onions was a stroke of genius on the part of the Almighty; there are other things equally good in life, some better, but they were 12,000 miles away.

Our *nasigorengs* were almost entirely rice, with little fish and no meat, but I still find, 30 years later, that with the addition of a little more of these things, *nasigoreng* can be a very good dish.

To make a good *nasigoreng*, you have to be able to cook your rice well. This is not a cookery book, but perhaps I should explain how we cooked dry rice. Take rice, put it in a saucepan with a well-fitting lid, add cold water to one finger-knuckle depth above the rice (I realise that I can be criticised as this measures a height rather than a volume, but it works for the average saucepan). Add a spoonful of salt, put the lid on tightly and cook over a very low flame. Do not disturb it, even avoid taking the lid off, for 45 minutes, at the end of which time, serve – or make a *nasigoreng* of it. According to the height of the flame, there will be a layer of slightly browned 'biscuit' lining the saucepan, but this is good to eat and is even better fried. The instructions one reads in books or hears on television about washing boiled rice in a colander under the tap to separate the grains! Rice is the staple carbohydrate food of Indonesia; the women all cook it excellently and many of them have never even seen a tap, let alone a colander. The nonsense that many cookery experts talk and write today is crystallised in this single fact. Has nobody ever thought to enquire how Indonesian women, who, after all, are the experts, do it?

In the quest for firewood and, for that matter, onions, the Dutch has a slight advantage over us. These things were not easy to come by and the Dutch troops, many of whom were half or wholly Indonesian, had a knowledge and capability of living off the countryside that our people could not hope to have. Almost magically, Indonesian troops could produce both of these commodities from an apparently quite unproductive terrain. They, of course, had an easier rapport with the local population if they could mix with them on working parties, and though these things seem unimportant so long afterwards, they were literally a life-and-death matter to us then.

Whenever there are two groups of people in a confined situation, there is the possibility of friction between them, simply because they are two groups. The British and Dutch at Haruku – or in any other prison camp – could have had this difficulty. That we did not is, I think, the result of several factors. Firstly, both sides were aware that it might happen and were careful to guard against it; secondly, and perhaps more important, we were united in loathing and despising the Japanese. We were ranged against a common enemy, which made us very conscious of the unwisdom of quarrelling among ourselves and removed any desire we might have had to do so. There were other considerations. In our situation as doctors, we were professional colleagues; likes and dislikes took second place, and we got on together. And there was Rudi Springer, a man whom everybody respected, colleagues and all with whom he came into contact. His nationality was unimportant: he was simply a good, kind, courageous, courteous and witty man. Nevertheless, by common and unspoken consent, the British and Dutch formed separate groups for private catering, so we lost out on firewood. No harsh word was ever spoken, but somebody else's onions do smell good cooking, when you have none for yourself.

Considering the circumstances, we were a disciplined body of men. We were in a unique situation: in order to survive at all, we had to behave as a coordinated group. Had there been any cracking of discipline within the camp itself, Heaven knows what would have happened, and it was greatly to the credit of the vast majority that there was not. It is usually considered that in order to impose discipline, there must be some system of punishments. Obviously, in our situation this was not possible, nor, fortunately, was it necessary. The Japanese had informed us perfectly clearly that anybody requiring punishment was to be handed over to them. This was quite unthinkable, so discipline was maintained by a combination of two things: the fact that nearly everybody realised that they had to conform if the camp was to run at all, and perhaps an appreciation of the men that the officers, in so far as they had authority, were trying to help. Personality entered into it as well. The situation was really rather an interesting one, because order had to be kept by the officers without any divine right of authority of all. Perhaps the most vitally important factor was that we knew each other, liked each other, and stood together.

Even though at no time was a transgressor reported to the Japanese, there were, nevertheless, occasions when they discovered some real or imagined offence for themselves. The beatings, personally performed by Mori before the whole camp on parade, that occurred on these occasions still sicken me in the memory. Men were killed by them; not immediately, but they died, clearly as a consequence of the injuries they received. Mori, once he started beating a man, appeared to lose his sanity. he was, in any case, an unstable man, being particularly fearsome at the time of the full moon. I most clearly remember a Canadian sergeant who was subjected to a particularly vicious beating for some matter (I cannot remember what) which was offensive to the Japanese. He stood up to it with immense fortitude: whenever he was knocked down, he stood straight up again. He never recovered from it and died some weeks later. I was with him at the time. Mori obviously intended the beating to be an example to us, but it had precisely the opposite effect of knitting us more closely together.

We did not, even in our most optimistic moments, really expect to survive. If we were not killed by starvation and squalor, we thought that the Japanese would get rid of us just as soon as our usefulness to them had ceased. There was no evidence at that time that we were regarded as anything other than a cheap labour force to be used as long as we survived, and the stories they told us of how the war was going suggested that they were confident of winning it in the Far Eastern theatre. So they did not see the need to conform with the normally accepted dictates of humanity because, if they were the winners, nobody could do much about it afterwards. We had had no news whatsoever except what they told us, and what they told us was a story of continuous victory. That they intended to kill us was probably right. If we were not starved to death, we could have been marched to death. We had no knowledge that this is what they intended, but it was apparent after the war that they did this in other places. In my opinion, there is no question at all that what spared us this fate at the end was the sudden cessation of hostilities following the Hiroshima and Nagasaki atomic bombs – but I am running ahead with my story. At that time, at Haruku, we kept our spirits up – and tried to give hope to the sick – by imagining that one day, without warning, a fleet of Allied destroyers would sail into the harbour and rescue us. After all – and equally improbably – this had happened when the prisoners were rescued from the German ship *Altmark* by the Navy, early in the war. I am sure that none of us really believed that this would happen, but if everybody pretends that he believes something strongly enough, the corporate pretence turns into hope.

Apart from this vague hope for the future, we found it wise not to look too far ahead. Experience had shown us that there was practically no limit to the degradation and misery that could be heaped upon us, so for my part – and I am sure others felt the same – I never looked beyond tomorrow evening. This divided one's life into manageable lumps. In fact, there were approximately 1,200 days.

Great thinkers in the past have often been ascetics, imposing starvation upon themselves. I found, and probably others shared my experience, that in a state of chronic starvation, one became very clear-headed. I am sure that I understood abstruse ideas more clearly (we had a book about relativity, so I was able to test this). I still had a little paper, a few paints and a brush, and the paintings that I was able to make at Haruku were better – far better – than I thought myself capable of, better than anything I had done before. At least, I have evidence of this as I managed to bring one or two of them home between the layers of my pack. Though I make no pretence of more than average skill, the concept of genius starving in an attic is not entirely a false picture. In one's debilitated state, the act of painting was completely exhausting. Each time, I was totally spent for the next two days.

We were running short of clothes. Each man had a pair of shorts and something, much patched, to cover his top half. Many had no hats. Our hair was shaved or cut extremely short as a precaution against infestation, so the absence of both hat and hair in the tropical sun might be thought to have been dangerous. Sunstroke, after all, was considered to be a real hazard in the tropics, so much so that in India, the British wore not only pith helmets but protection for the spine as well. I can vouch, from personal experience, that this is simply a myth. Men went out to work day in, day out, with head shaved, neck and back bare (most wore no shirts), and whatever our troubles, sunstroke was not one of them. I had had a sola topee for some time. It had two advantages: it was cool and it protected me from serious injury when set upon and hit about the head by an angry Japanese. After it disintegrated, I wore nothing on my head – for years. My observations on sunstroke, I would emphasise, do not apply to heatstroke, which is quite different, being due to excessive heat to which the body is unable to adjust – a dangerous condition, not uncommon in ships' stokers in the tropics.

Some of us grew beards, having no razors; some had managed to raid an American store early on and had provided themselves – as I had – with a Schick Injector, a razor designed so that each new blade, when it is put in, ejects the old one, which cannot then be put back. I managed to get myself about 100 blades and found that by a simple modification, filing off a small catch on the razor, it was possible for the blade to be taken out, washed and sharpened. I shaved twice a week or so. My 100 blades lasted me for about 350 shaves and, so far as I remember, I had a few left at the end. I go into this detail because Mori at one stage started to grow a beard. After a week or two, it was quite evident to him (and to us) that his was not a very good beard. So he ordered all men in the camp with beards to remove them. After the lapse of a decent interval, he removed his. We extracted a good deal of humour from this situation.

The canvas boots we wore when we came to Haruku had long since worn out and there were difficulties about going barefoot. Not only were minor injuries to the legs and feet liable to turn into shocking ulcers, particularly those made by coral (and this was a coral island), but the undergrowth contained many sago trees. Sago is extracted from the inside of the trunk of the tree after it has been cut down, but when growing, it produces thorns all round it which are the sharpest, longest, hardest, most barbaric thorns I have ever seen. A man unwarily stepping on one of these with a bare foot could have his foot completely transfixed by it; we had to deal with many injuries of this sort. So it was necessary to wear some sort of shoe if possible, and we became skilled at making wooden platform shoes with a strap, fixed on slightly obliquely. The whole success of this type of shoe, that is, its ability to stay on, depended on the exact position of the strap and its angle in relation to the foot. Such shoes are commonplace among young women now but were not, as far as I know, worn in the West at that time.

Watches and gold rings were currency at Haruku, simply because the Japanese wanted them. I suspect that Mori was the only one into whose hands most, if not all, finally found their way as he seemed to have absolute power over all the guards, who, clearly, were frightened of him. The Japanese did not actually steal watches; instead, they exchanged them for minute amounts of food – a few papayas, some sugar and some peanuts. Obviously, if a man was starving, he reached the point where the prospect of a single blow-out transcended everything else and he gave up his watch. This is important because, of course, nobody would have retained his watch and starved to death, but the point at which it was given up was crucial. I kept mine until later on – and it undoubtedly saved my life.

Dead men had signet rings and wedding rings, and I regret that there was a certain amount of trafficking in these to the Japanese. But, as far as I know, only one individual stole them from the mortuary. Naturally, in any community of 2000 men, there must be one or two with criminal tendencies, but apart from this, the traded rings were not stolen. As with watches, a ring was a commodity which could be used when a man felt he required extra food for survival. Many a man, at one time or another, came to me in great concern because his wife had given him his ring, possibly it was his last material connection with her, and he was loth to part with it. One can understand this, as the prospect of continuing family life after the war was over, was the only thing that sustained many men – most of us, in fact. One's advice in this situation was quite clear: his wife would unquestionably prefer him to come home without his ring than not to come home at all – but it was a very serious issue at the time.

I was spared having to make the decision for myself over the signet ring Emmie had given me. One day, I had dived into the water over the coral reef to try to catch myself a fish, and I was by now so thin that the ring slipped off and I never saw it again. Looking back, it is extraordinary how desolate I felt at losing this one remaining present from Emmie. How clearly I understood the feelings of the men in their dilemma.

This brings me to the whole question of cooperation with the Japanese. There was a clear distinction between cooperation for the public good and cooperation for purely personal gain, particularly if that gain was at the expense of the camp's rations. There were sometimes difficult points of distinction, but usually the issue was easily solved. We had craftsmen with useful skills in the camp, particularly a watchmaker and a carpenter.

It may seem strange that a watchmaker should find a use

70

for his services in such a place, but those men who had not yet traded their watches for food required them to be kept in order against the day when they did, so that they kept their value. Mori, making a collection of prisoners' watches, also needed them to be kept going as they represented a considerable amount of capital, and for this reason the watchmaker, who had managed to find a magnifying glass somewhere, was allowed to have a small room to himself and excused from the outside working party. So he worked for us and he worked for the Japanese, but there was never any question of where his heart lay. he was far from well anyway, and I am sure he received very little payment in kind as he never really recovered his health after dysentery.

How different was the behaviour of the carpenter. Though his job was to use his skill for us, he soon learned that working for the Japanese would provide him with unlimited rice – from our ration. he rapidly became fat, so fat that he quivered as he walked, and because his fatness was due to white rice, he was on the verge of serious deficiency. Not long after this, we were all to be subjected to a period of intense starvation. The scraggy, skeletal men were by this time so conditioned to privation that we coped far better than the few fat ones. Our carpenter died, still fat, within 48 hours of the start of the cut in our rations – and was unmourned.

The problem of what to do with the very few people – there were possibly two, or at the most three – who cooperated with the Japanese in this way was insoluble. They, alone among the prisoners, were the ones who deserved to be reported to the Japanese for punishment, but had we done this, the Japanese, of course, would have done nothing; these men were their blue-eyed boys. Justice caught up soon enough with those who grew fat by collaboration: they died. I lost track of the man who traded the wedding rings of the dead, but I understood that as soon as the Japanese capitulated some two years later, his companions in the camp gave him a thrashing he would never forget. I have no proof of this, but if true, it was well-deserved rough justice.

The cookhouse staff grew fat. This was really inevitable as

71

they had access to unlimited food: rice, vegetables and meat. Human nature being as it is, it would have been strange, however reprehensible it may seem, if they had not indulged themselves at our expense. They did not mix much with the rest of the camp; one can see why. When taxed with their well-nourished state, they claimed that cooks got fat anyway – a likely tale. On a Japanese holiday in 1944, the guards decided that they would like to see a football match. It had to be called off because the cooks were the only team with sufficient strength to play; everyone else was too weak. Many of the cooks, unused to deprivation, succumbed rapidly when later they were subjected to starvation. The brutal truth was that at that time, at Haruku, anybody who by some illicit means came by extra rations and ate unwisely – that is, ate an excess of polished rice – was doomed. None of us was to know then that the ration position would become infinitely worse, and the strange paradox was continually being brought to our attention that skinny men – not, of course, those wasted to skin and bone by illness, but men thin from want – did better than the fatter ones when subjected to still further privation. I also formed the impression that men thin by nature (as I was) were better able to resist starvation than those naturally well-covered.

There was another way of legitimately supplementing our rations besides the camp shop – theft from the Japanese. Some of the men worked near enough to the Japanese ration store to keep an eye on it and seize an occasion when the guard was not looking to win something on the side. Tinned meat was the objective. If successful, they would take a whole crate, bury it nearby and remove a tin or two as needed. They ran a great risk of a severe beating if caught, but surprisingly this did not happen very often. This extra food made a significant difference to the health of a few men, and in a way compensated for the rations the Japanese were using to pay their one or two favourites.

We had a little tobacco. The only sort we could get legally, from the camp shop, was the debris – the larger veins – left over from the leaves from which cigars had been made, cigar-making being a local industry in some parts of Indonesia. The method of making our mixture smokable was to soak the veins in water until soft, beat them flat with a hammer or other heavy blunt object, cut them into shreds and, while it was still moist, put the resulting mixture into an airtight tin with, if one had it, a small piece of banana skin. Cigarettes made from this were not very satisfactory as it was too granular, but we had a little teak and we carved pipes. There were some broken-down black Bakelite car batteries about, and we used them to make mouthpieces. I still have some of this material embedded in my thumb; my knife slipped when I was carving one.

Lighting our pipes could be a problem: the guards had matches but did not see fit to give us many, so we used an ingenious type of tinder-box which the Dutch knew about and which worked on the same principle as the diesel engine. A hole about 5 cm deep and 1 cm wide was drilled into a small piece of teak and a circular wooden rod found which exactly fitted the hole. It had to be a tight fit but not so tight that it could not easily be withdrawn. The end of the rod was carved into a slightly concave shape. A small piece of tinder – carefully dried, fluffy vegetable material (hairs from the leaf of a palm) – was put into the hole, the rod inserted and given a sharp blow to drive it to the bottom – or nearly to the bottom – of the hole. The sudden compression of air in the cavity so raised the temperature, that the tinder, tipped out immediately, was smouldering. It was placed on more tinder and nursed while it smoked and finally flamed.

There was another sort of tobacco which we called golden glory. This was stored by the Japanese for their own use in discs about 8 cm across and 2 cm thick. It was kept in the store in bamboo tubes – the bamboo is a most extraordinarily useful plant as the natural form of the stem is a tube with partitions every so often, so it can be used as a container or made into water-pipes and gutters. Its uses are almost unlimited. It is so hard and rigid that it even makes passable daggers and knives. Some 10 or 15 discs of golden glory were stored in each bamboo tube and there were many stacked in the store.

73

Our men kept themselves supplied with it when nobody was looking, leaving each tube with a disc of tobacco at each end, but none in the middle, so that to a casual observer they still appeared full. The only reason I can think of why the Japanese did not suspect that they were being systematically robbed was that they themselves were indulging in so much racketeering that checks were not encouraged – or were impossible. By the standards of those days, it was excellent tobacco, but as I have given up smoking since I have now no way of making a comparison. Occasionally a few cigarettes came our way. The brand name was Silver City – and they tasted of mildew.

It was always evident to us, as it would have been clear to anyone else in the same situation, that to run our own gardens and grow our own vegetables would have solved many of our difficulties. Of course, to be useful, such a garden would have to be fairly large and would require a number of men to cultivate it. The Japanese, in the earliest part of our stay, steadfastly refused to allow men, even the walking sick, to stay back from the outside working party to grow food; indeed, they would not even allow men to stay back for sanitary control duties. The sheer short-sightedness of this policy staggers one, but the Japanese could not be convinced – or, as I have said before, they may have been afraid to have us all fit: their conduct later, on the journey back to Java, most strongly suggested this. If we had been allowed to grow vegetables (as was demonstrated in Changi Gaol, where I was to go much later on), our health would have been immeasurably improved and the working parties might well have been increased.

After the most seriously ill men left us, we were finally allowed to try to make a garden. Clearing scrub was heavy and unpleasant work. Sago trees with their thorns were all over the place, and dysentery patients on the verge of deficiency disease found the work hard; but the better convalescents, and officers not on duty for the outside working party on that day, finally cleared a large space, about five acres. The labour problem in the garden was always difficult, and many men who should have been resting had to work there. As much control was kept of this as possible by the medical staff. Every convalescent man was examined daily for signs of deterioration, particularly early heart failure, and many, I feel, benefited in the end from the light work they did in the gardens. But another difficulty we had to face was that as soon as the garden working party was sufficiently big for each man to do just as much work as he was capable of doing, Mori and a party of Japanese would descend and take many of the men away for outside work.

The soil was fertile. The crops to be grown were ordained by the Japanese, who took the larger share for themselves (which was the only reason why the gardens were allowed at all). The chief were tapioca, sweet potatoes and onions, and a few peanuts, tomatoes and small chillies. A few men tried to make private gardens but had to give up because of lack of time and strength. Tomatoes grew very well. Before the latrine over the sea was made, during one night of torrential rain, the camp was temporarily flooded. Water poured down a ditch beside our hut, converting it into a deep gully. All the latrines in the camp overflowed, their contents rushing down the gully with the flood water. The floods subsided next morning, but so many tomato seeds were brought down from the latrines that in the next few weeks we had a very large crop growing wild up the sides of the gully.

The latrine over the sea had stopped fresh cases of dysentery occurring but we were finding more and more men with vitamin deficiency signs, the most serious of which was the partial blindness caused by optic neuritis. A green bean called *katchang idjoe* was a rich source of the vitamin B complex and we could sometimes buy a sack or two of it, but the amount was too small to help. A brown bean, *katchang kedele*, was more easily obtainable but I found it totally indigestible, even ground to a pulp. Nevertheless, a useful protein-rich food called *tempeh* could be made from it by fungal action.

* * *

The position was extremely serious: such help as the garden

75

gave us, though it improved the flavour and quality of our food, had come too late and was too little to prevent fresh cases of optic neuritis occurring, and there was a real risk that all, or nearly all, of us would go partially blind. We were most fortunate in having with us an expert plant physiologist, Dr (now Professor) Leslie J Audus, who was in the RAF as a radio officer. We had many times discussed the question of producing yeast – one of the richest natural sources of the vitamin B complex – even before we came to Haruku, and now, with all of us suffering some degree of B complex deficiency, something like yeast was vital to us. In order to explain what happened, I must go back in time to the days at Surabaya, before we set off for Haruku. I was not with Leslie Audus at the start of this work as I was with the working party at Semarang, so I have drawn on his own account of it from his paper 'Biology behind the Barbed Wire'[2] for details of his early experiments.

Yeast is a single-celled plant which obtains its energy in order to multiply, not directly from the sun as green plants do, but from the breakdown of sugar, carbon dioxide gas and alcohol being formed in the process. The source of the sugar may be fruit, as in wine-making, sugar added to the dough in bread-making (the bubbles of carbon dioxide making the bread rise), or germinating the grains, as in the production of whisky. When grain is used, the starch present in it must first be broken down into sugars. This happens (by the action of complex substances called enzymes) when the grain germinates. Yeast therefore will grow in a solution of the products of germination of unpolished, living rice. These are glucose, some maltose, and simple nitrogenous compounds. Polished rice, being incapable of germination, cannot be used as the embryo has been removed. The native population of Java knew how to break down the starch of polished rice into sugars by allowing a mould to grow on it – a special sort of

[2]Audus, L J, 'Biology Behind the Barbed Wire', *Discovery* Vol. 7 No. 7, 1946 (p.211).

mould. The rice so broken down is then fermented with yeast, making a dish called *ragi* rich in vitamins of the B complex. I feel that this explanatory note is necessary if the ingenious work of Leslie Audus is to be understood by those untrained in these matters. I am fortunate that Professor Audus has recently gone over in greater detail the methods he devised and I have therefore added this information to my account.

In the preliminary work at Surabaya, the apparatus used consisted of tin cans, cisterns, an old Dutch army cooker and a thermometer made of a piece of glass tubing and some mercury. Electrical engineers were available and the camp had an electricity supply. Amazingly, electric heaters, thermostatically controlled though primitive, were made there. From these bits and pieces, a steriliser with an immersion heater and an incubator with a conduction heater were constructed. Petri dishes (a type of dish used in bacteriological culture) were found in the dispensary stock, agar (a jelly-like material used for culture media) could be bought as it was a Japanese food-article, and hydrochloric acid (to produce 'invert' sugar – a sugar formed by the breakdown of cane sugar into simpler sugars, necessary for the multiplication of yeast) was available in small quantities. The dispensary carried a stock of the materials needed to make Fehling's solution, really intended for urine-testing, but in this case used for quantitative sugar estimation, so all the necessary materials and equipment could be made or obtained. I emphasise that all this happened in Java, civilized by any standards.

The first problem was to find a suitable strain of yeast. here, the Javanese *ragi* came to our aid and turned out to be a valuable source of active yeast (indeed, in the way things have of happening, the desire of the Javanese population for *ragi* was undoubtedly connected with its richness in the vitamin B complex due to its yeast content). Maize was available in some quantity at this time in the relative plenty of Java and, germinated, was the first medium used for growing yeast.

The maize was first soaked for two days in water which was frequently changed. It was then left between damp sacks until the sprouts on the grains were between 2 and 3 cm long. This degree of development was found to correspond with the greatest production of the enzyme diastase, responsible for conversion of the starch of the grain into sugar. The maize was now ground down to a coarse paste, mixed with water and incubated for 15 hours. Sugar determinations (using Fehling's solution) showed that, by this time, 60 per cent of the starch had been converted to sugar, giving a sugar concentration of 8 per cent. The liquid was then filtered, sterilised and allowed to cool in sterilised petrol tins, after which it was inoculated with a pure yeast culture. Strict attention to aseptic techniques was necessary as otherwise it was found that there was a serious overgrowth of the lactic acid bacillus, greatly reducing the amount of yeast that could be produced – but even the lactic acid bacillus was to become our friend later.

The pure yeast culture was prepared in the following manner. A small quantity of *ragi* was smuggled into the camp by the outside working party and inoculated on to a nutrient jelly made from *agar*. Three vigorous yeast strains which grew from it were isolated and grown in pure culture. Having been isolated (that is, obtained free from any contaminating organism) the yeast was grown in tubes of a liquid nutrient medium made from sterilised maize filtrate enriched with invert sugar made by the action of dilute hydrochloric acid on cane sugar, the sugar content of this medium being adjusted to 15 per cent. Here, the yeast remained for four days, after which these tubes were inoculated into bottles of similarly enriched medium.

Again after four days, these cultures were used to inoculate the petrol tins of pure maize-malt filtrate, known as 'wort'. After two or three days, a sludge settled to the bottom of the tins. This was yeast. It was given to patients selected by the medical staff, those with optic neuritis receiving most, though the few cases at this time in Java were mild compared to those we should see later at Haruku.

Our supplies of maize, even in Java, soon became short, so the method that had been developed became impracticable and another substance had to be found to make a medium which did not rely on maize. Rice was relatively plentiful but, as I have said, polished rice is dead, cannot be germinated and cannot therefore be used for the production of yeast unless the starch in it can first be converted to sugar. Here again, *ragi* provided the answer as the change we were looking for took place in its production. So steamed rice (after cooling) was inoculated with *ragi* under sterile conditions and after five days was found to be covered with a pink mould. Its exact species was unknown but it was probably a mixture of at least two. The whole was then mixed with water and incubated for 15 hours to allow the diastase which, it was hoped, the mould had liberated, to act on the starch. The result was a fluid with a sugar content sufficiently high for it to be used as a wort to grow yeast. Thus, then, was the preliminary work done by Leslie Audus in Java in anticipation of just the plight in which we now found ourselves – and at this very moment (the same moment when my artificial hand was beginning to work) the camp was split up.

Those of us going to Haruku were incredibly fortunate that Leslie Audus was to come with us. He secreted in his kit a yeast culture (not the pure one; one of his co-workers had that) and the thermometer they had used. This proved most useful in the isolation of the most 'efficient' fungus to use when finally he was able to start trying to produce yeast at Haruku, but then it was broken and he had to judge temperatures with his elbow.

I have already described our arrival at Haruku. Obviously, any sort of yeast production, starting again from scratch, was quite impossible during the few months that followed. The majority of the men were sick (including Leslie Audus himself), little camp organisation was possible and any available men who could have taken part in yeast production were forced to go out and work on the airstrip by the Japanese.

At the end of September 1943, after the ferocity of our epidemic had died down and the party of very sick men had left us, some Dutch prisoners were brought in by the Japanese from another island. One of them, Dr (now Professor) JC ten Houten, a plant pathologist, had succeeded in producing a poor culture of yeast which was considered to have been of some value in the prevention of deficiency symptoms. His method was to ferment a mixture of cane sugar, rice washings and coconut water (so-called 'milk' from germinating coconuts, known to be rich in diastase). This method did not appear practicable for bulk production, but as our need of yeast was greater than ever before, Leslie Audus and Dr ten Houten started work together to try to devise a method based on the previous work in Java.

The position regarding apparatus was far worse than at Surabaya (where it had been relatively good). Vessels were extremely scarce, there was no electricity, and the only scientific apparatus was a microscope and a Thoma Haemocytometer (a special microscope slide with very finely ruled lines on it to enable cells to be counted under the microscope). I cannot think why the Japanese saw fit to bring these unlikely pieces of apparatus, which are used in the diagnosis of blood disease, if indeed they did. It is more likely that they were brought from Java by a Dutch pharmacist called Papenrecht, but however they came, these two pieces of equipment were to prove invaluable as they could be used for accurate yeast cell counts, to give early warning of dwindling production. Fortunately, some locally made ketchup had been delivered to the camp in large earthenware jars reminiscent of Ali-Baba – so-called 'carboys'. These turned out to be most useful in yeast production, as home-made wooden vessels, the only alternative, could not be adequately sterilised and very soon became heavily infected with lactic acid bacilli, inhibiting the growth of yeast. With all possible precautions, the lactic acid bacilli at one time became so vigorous that they practically jeopardised the whole yeast production. Of this, and the means used to combat it, more will be said later.

Leslie Audus first turned his attention to the isolation of a mould which would break down the starch of rice to form materials suitable for the growth of yeast (no *ragi* was available to enable us to replace our lost mould culture). A bowl of steamed rice, cool, of course, was exposed to the air for 15 minutes, covered with a damp cloth sterilised by boiling and left for two days. Many moulds grew upon it, but one grew

80

well and was recognised as being the one used by the Javanese in the production of *ragi*. It was isolated in pure culture by inoculating it under aseptic conditions on to cooled, freshly steamed rice. We now had the means of making a sugar solution from rice of about 5 to 8 per cent concentration.

The Japanese, of course, were as fierce as ever in turning men out of the camp for the outside working party and would not have allowed men to stay in to make yeast, had it not been for one thing: a by-product of yeast growth was alcohol, and the idea of free daily alcohol appealed to the Japanese, so yeast production was allowed. At other times and in other places the order of importance of these two aspects is reversed – we live in a strange world. The Japanese, however, were afraid of what the alcohol might do to us, should we get hold of it. Indeed, a Japanese medical officer had to be convinced, Leslie Audus told me, that the sterilisation process, to which our yeast ration was finally submitted, removed the alcohol, which in fact it did not.

Leslie Audus and his small team finally evolved the following method of propagating yeast. Freshly steamed rice from the cookhouse was allowed to cool. Shallow rectangular trays about one metre long, the sides made of wood and the bottom of taut sacking, were lined with fresh green leaves. Some of the ground-up pure culture of the grey mould already isolated was sprinkled on to the layer of leaves, and a layer of rice, rather more than one inch thick, was spread on this. A further sprinkling of ground-up mould was put on the rice, and the whole covered with fresh leaves. Thus a sandwich was made, with a layer of rice in the middle. On each surface of this was a layer of mould, and outside, top and bottom, was a layer of fresh leaves. Humidity could be regulated by removing a few of the leaves from the top.

These trays were stacked in a warm corner and left for 24 hours, during which time the rice became warmer than the surrounding air. The top layer of leaves was then removed and the trays left for another 14 to 16 hours, during which time the rice with the fungus growing on it became a matted mass and could be taken out of the tray practically in one piece.

81

These rice mats were broken up, put into the carboys, which were of about 25 litres capacity, and warm water poured on to them, the temperature being carefully adjusted so that, when the vessel was full, it was about 60 °C. The carboy was stoppered with a wooden bung and put into a home-made haybox – an old tea chest packed with sacks – and left for 22 hours, after which, the temperature was about 40 degrees. The contents of the carboys – a solution of the various breakdown products of the rice after its digestion by the fungus, with a sugar content of about 5 per cent – were then filtered, sterilised by boiling, and left in iron cooking drums covered with sterile cloths to await inoculation of the yeast. No means were available of isolating a pure culture, so we had to be content with a mixture of strains obtained from the surface of bananas. Inoculation of our mixed yeast was performed in three stages. Firstly, it was inoculated into sterilised bottles of the rice wort enriched with invert sugar. Miraculously, a little hydrochloric acid for making invert sugar had survived. The sugar content of this mixture was about 15 per cent. After two or three days, the yeast culture was used to inoculate stone jars of the same medium, which were again left for two or three days. This second culture was then used for inoculating the iron drums of rice wort. Fermentation in the drums took some 48 hours, after which the fluid was sterilised and issued in 50 ml doses to all men in the camp. Three times this quantity was given to those with gross signs of vitamin B deficiency. The total daily output, in full production, was about two kilograms of moist yeast per day for the camp population of about a thousand men. The by-product, which was the price we paid to the Japanese, was six bottles of a raw, sour, turbid alcoholic brew.

Two serious difficulties arose in the course of this work. The first was the ever-present trouble from over-growth of the lactic acid bacillus, and the second, that we inevitably ran out of hydrochloric acid. The first problem was to a great extent solved, as it was found that the bacillus liked a higher temperature for growth than did yeast. By placing the iron drums containing the sterile wort – that is, the fluid, filtered and sterilised, formed by the action of the mould on the rice – in the river nearby to cool before yeast inoculation, the temperature could be brought down to 25 degrees, which allowed the yeast to grow while tending to inhibit the lactic acid bacillus (which was a contaminant of our stock yeast culture). The second difficulty, the failure of the hydrochloric acid supply for the production of invert sugar to enrich the medium on which the yeast was 'started', was solved after a great deal of trouble by using our old enemy, the lactic acid bacillus, in separate culture to make lactic acid for us, which it would do, in favourable circumstances, up to a concentration of 1.5 per cent. This lactic acid, Leslie Audus found, was satisfactory in the production of invert sugar.

The foregoing episode is, to my mind, a triumph; a triumph against, all the time, seemingly overwhelming odds; a triumph on the part of Leslie Audus and Dr ten Houten and, I feel, a triumph which has been insufficiently recognised. Almost alone, they were responsible for saving the eyesight of hundreds of men. No fresh cases of optic neuritis occurred after we went on to the yeast ration, and all manner of changes due to vitamin B deficiency diseases that were reversible began to improve. Unfortunately, optic neuritis itself, once established, was not reversible.

It is interesting to reflect that all of this was only possible because the Japanese received from it six bottles of alcoholic drink each day. The frailties of the human race can sometimes confer unexpected benefits. Just as unknown and unsung Chinese prostitutes saved our health at Semarang, so the liking of the Japanese guards for a tipple saved our eyesight – and, to a great extent, our health – at Haruku.

5

HARUKU III. CORAL

During the first half of 1944 we were ordered by the Japanese to dig a well at the corner of the parade-ground in the camp, just beside the window of the hut where the doctors and other officers lived. We, the medical staff, protested that with old latrine trenches all around the area, there would be seepage of infected material into the subsoil throughout that part of the camp and any water that might collect in the well would be extremely dangerous to drink. But this in no way deterred the Japanese and it was evident that something else was afoot. About six of our men were detailed to do the digging; the work was not hard as the soil was sandy. As they got deeper, the shape of the hole had the effect of amplifying the conversation of the two who were at the bottom and their shouted comments to those at the top who were hauling up the bucketfuls of sand. As with troops anywhere, the commonest adjective is one derived from a four-letter Anglo-Saxon word, and on this particular day every second word seemed to be an expletive. Finally, a fellow officer, 'Bulgy' Blackwood (now, alas, no longer bulgy), a journalist by peacetime trade and a good raconteur who kept us happy with his stories, both real and apocryphal, called out – and I use the convention invented by the late Neville Shute which I hope is clearly understood – 'If you chaps stopped saying "muck", you would say muck-all.'

The purpose of the well and the general smartening-up of the camp that went with it became apparent in the next few weeks: we were to be inspected by a high-ranking Japanese officer. It did not dawn upon us, or at any rate, upon me at the time, but the very fact that the Japanese required the camp to be inspected suggested that they were becoming sensitive to the attitude of the world regarding their treatment of prisoners, and they would not have felt like this if they were sure of winning the war – they simply would not have cared. In retrospect, it is now clear that this was the first sign they showed us that they knew that their actions might finally be submitted to world judgement.

Before the inspection of the camp took place, another remarkable event occurred. There were, as far as I knew at that time, no cattle on the island, goats and their milk, chickens, fish and eggs being the protein food of the local population. But, evidently, cattle had to be on view at the time of the inspection, no doubt to give the impression that meat and even dairy products were available for the prisoners, so one day, several barge-loads of miserable cows were brought to the jetty, unloaded and put to graze on a patch of grass near the camp. The inspection by the officer took place, with considerable pomp and ceremony – and drawing-in of breath through closed teeth – and the next day, the cattle were driven down to the jetty, reloaded on to the barges and taken away. We did not see them again, and certainly none of the prisoners had beef for supper. Whether the Japanese did, I do not know. No doubt, photographs of the inspection became available for propaganda purposes.

At about this time, we lost our beloved steamroller. Perhaps it was required for work on another island, or perhaps it was too valuable just to leave there and was shipped to Java. Whatever the reason, a ship arrived offshore, and two barges were brought to the end of the jetty, lashed together and tied to the wooden piers. The steamroller boiler was filled, wood was collected, an Indonesian driver was found – probably the one who had originally driven it – and for the first time for years the roller got up steam. The intention of the Japanese was, it appeared clear, to wait until high tide, run the steamroller along the jetty, drive it over the end to a drop of perhaps two feet on to the barges and float it out to the ship,

85

which had cranes to hoist it aboard. It was a crazy idea: the jetty was a flimsy wooden structure built for nothing heavier than a handcart and it was evident to all of us – we were all in the camp that day for some reason – that here were the makings of high drama. But amazingly, despite the hopes of a thousand men – we all hoped to see the operation go wrong and the steamroller plunge into the sea, preferably with a big bang – the heavy machine trundled down the jetty, the whole structure rocking from side to side, and by some miracle the barges held together and remained afloat when the roller landed on them. It was towed out to sea without any mishap. We had been so looking forward to the bang, though we were sufficiently charitable to hope that, had it happened, the driver would have jumped clear. My mind went back to Semarang and the railway laid across the marshy airfield. Clearly, a source of the military strength of the Japanese was their ability to get away with makeshift methods. No European in his right mind would have attempted to move a steamroller like that.

* * *

Although acute dysentery was no longer a problem after September 1943, we had other troubles in addition to the vitamin deficiencies from which all to a greater or lesser extent suffered; in fact, nearly all our medical difficulties were related to malnutrition. We suffered from ulcers. We called them 'coral' ulcers because they almost always started from a scratch or abrasion made by coral. My impression was that it was not necessary for the coral to be alive to cause an ulcer; living coral is found only in the sea, but the island was composed of dead coral thrown up by volcanic action, and scratches sustained at work on the airstrip seemed nearly as troublesome as those the men got when they paddled in the sea and came into contact with living coral. Rudi Springer and I ran a clinic for the treatment of these ulcers – mainly in the evening when the men came back from work – and in the six-month period from January to June 1944, there were literally thousands of attendances from the thousand men in the camp.

86

The ulcers were extremely painful – as I discovered myself – and spread rapidly round the scratch from which they started, some becoming fully five inches across and eroding down to the bone of the leg or foot, exposing the tendons as they spread. One, at least, was fatal. We had very little with which to cure them, but we did have marked success with two forms of treatment. For all but the largest, we would mop them as clean as possible with sterilised cloth (afterwards boiled and saved for further use), then pour in some crystals of potassium permanganate. After a day or two of this, we poured in a little iodoform powder (the smell of which, for me, always evoked the Infirmary at Christ's Hospital). Usually, this worked if the ulcer had not become too large, but both potassium permanganate and iodoform were in very short supply – simply that which we had brought by chance, and a little foresight, with us – and we had the agonising task of selecting patients for the only method we had which worked reasonably quickly. Those ulcers that were not quite so bad we simply had to mop out and treat with salt-water compresses. Nobody, so far as I know, ever grumbled if he was not selected for our really effective treatment, but this was the spirit of the men.

For the worst ulcers, our treatment had to be quite horrible. We had a very small amount of general anaesthetic saved against the need for major surgery, so any surgical procedures upon ulcers had to be carried out without anaesthetics (local anaesthetics, of which we had a small supply, would not have been effective). Our treatment of the most severe spreading ulcers was to scrape away the diseased tissue with what is surgically called a sharp spoon – and it was just that, a small, solidly built spoon with a sharp edge. The agony of this requires no description. The patient was given something to hold on to, was expected to swear as much as he wanted, and was also given a cigarette made of stolen golden glory. Amazingly, the patients put up with this, partly because the pain of the ulcer, untreated, was so bad that anything, even temporary agony, was worthwhile to gain relief. One untoward effect was upon myself and, no doubt, on Springer as well: the strain of doing this was such that, in one's undernourished state, it was difficult not to pass out. A chair had to be handy. This experience made it very clear what surgery must have been like before the days of anaesthetics.

We had a use for our carefully saved general anaesthetic. By 1944, Allied bombers occasionally came over, particularly at the time of the full moon. Mori's moods were bad enough at the full moon anyway and the risk of being bombed only made them worse, but our delight at seeing our own people – albeit from the receiving end – knew no bounds. Perhaps, we thought, they knew we were there – perhaps they might even come and fetch us. In fact, the net result for us was that we had to dig deep shelters for the Japanese. In one raid – by day – bombers came over and dropped their load near our camp boundary. There was no reason that we could fathom why they should have done this unless they did in fact know we were there and wanted to improve our spirits, but the tragedy was that they hit the native village. Some were killed and a young girl had her arm blown off. She was brought to us to patch up and we used some of our precious anaesthetic. I think she did well (we hardly saw her again) but it all seemed so unnecessary. In this one tiny incident was a demonstration of the futility of war. These were simple people, living up to then in near-paradise and harming nobody. We had seen enough suffering and our compassion was fully aroused. In our deprived state, we found it particularly poignant that the victim should have been a pretty young girl.

In June 1944 we left Haruku, suddenly and with very little warning.

It is now evident that the Japanese were retreating and needed our services elsewhere, but we were not to know this at the time. We were simply told, one evening, 'All men leave 5 o'clock tomorrow morning. All men take what they can carry.' During the last nine months of our stay, after the party of seriously ill men had left, after the latrine over the sea had been made, after we had the gardens, and, particularly, after Leslie Audus' yeast ration was introduced, only 45 of our company died, including the 20 whom we had considered too ill to travel when the ships with the sick left. This compared with

370 deaths during our first four months, when dysentery raged, sanitary facilities were deplorable and we had no gardens or yeast. We left behind us 415 dead, buried above the shoreline of this truly beautiful island.

As we moved off from the camp, a strange thing happened. Beside the road, hidden in the bushes in the half-light, the local population had turned out and were playing a tune on bamboo pipes – the tune which has the words, 'When the bloody war is over, Oh! how happy I shall be'. One will never know whether they chose this tune because of the singularly appropriate words or whether it was a happy chance because the tune is also that of the delightful Salvation Army hymn 'Jesus wants me for a sunbeam' and they had clearly been visited by Dutch missionaries. As they understood almost no English, it is probably that it was a happy accident, possibly the happiest accident of a lifetime. Or perhaps – engaging thought – they had heard the men singing it as they marched to work and thought they went to work singing hymns. It was clearly an act of sympathy, of solidarity, because they too had had their share of maltreatment by the Japanese. It was a touching and moving experience.

6

AMBON

We divided into two parties, 650, said to be the fitter among us, going to work in the harbour on the island of Ambon, and the rest returning from Ambon to Java. I was in the Ambon working party. We were quartered in huts infested with malarial mosquitoes, and even though most – or all – had mosquito nets, the evenings, when we had to be about the camp for our evening meal, were the dangerous time and nearly everybody went down with malaria. Fortunately, it was of benign tertian type or few of us would have survived.

The job for which we had been brought to the island was to load ships with stores in the dock. Ambon, a small town, has a splendid natural harbour and was a staging-post for the Japanese in the islands all around. It was by now clear to us that they were pulling out – retreating – which was, of course, most encouraging for us: we did not really expect to see the end but it was nice to know that our side was winning.

Each day, the working party went to the harbour. There were crates of tinned meat among the store they loaded, and the men became very expert at recognising them by the Japanese characters on the side. The crane they were using was small, loading the crates one at a time, and was operated by one of our people. Whenever a crate of meat was spotted, it was let down rather too hard on to the floor of the hold so that it smashed. Our people down in the hold would quickly dismantle it, throw the smashed wood over the side and secrete the tins of meat out of sight. Some of them would be eaten at the time, but the men still had the problem of transporting those left over back to the camp for their mates, particularly those down with malaria, and of having some in store for a rainy day. There was a slight difficulty in smuggling the contraband tins into the camp, because concealment was impossible. By now, nearly everyone had run out of clothes, their only garments being wooden sandals and a strange affair, intended as underwear (and issued as such to the Japanese troops), which consisted of a strip of white cotton material about 9 inches wide and 24 inches long with a tape sewn to one end long enough to go round the waist and tie in a bow. To wear it, one simply placed the end of the cotton strip with the tape attached in the small of the back, brought the two ends of the tape forward round the waist and tied them together in front. The cotton strip was now hanging down at the back. This was brought forward under the crotch and slid beneath the tape, already tied, in front. The excess hung down at the front for decency. As may be imagined, it had no pockets, but it could be made to hang down as a sort of sling under the crotch and it was in this sling that tins of meat were carried back into the camp. it rather interfered with one's style of walking and the sight of a few hundred men marching back to the camp, some with tins of meat so slung, can well be imagined. At this point luck was in our favour: our guards were not very well off for rations themselves, so a sort of unspoken agreement was made. Our people were not punished for stealing the meat and bringing it into the camp; instead, every few days, the tins were taken away from them by the guard for their own use. Then, for a day or two, until they had run out, they took no more tins from our men, so it was still worth while to bring them in. The addition of this illicit protein to our diet was extremely valuable, indeed vital. It enabled some of us – unfortunately, nothing like all – to stand up to the rigours to come because, though we did not know it, our worst time was only a few weeks away.

Not only did the men become skilled at recognising cases of meat, they also split open any case likely to contain medicines. With a serious outbreak of malaria on our hands and no drugs to treat it except for a lamentably small supply of

91

quinine from the Japanese, this was of immense value to us. One day, when the problem had become acute, the men found and split open (after I had issued an appeal) a whole crate of bottles of quinine, and everybody working on that ship, so far as I know, brought back a bottle – it almost appeared to be an intervention of Fate. The parade of prisoners as they came in must have been quite a sight, each man carrying a bulky bottle of 500 quinine tablets slung under his crotch, though I did not see them come in as I was busy with the sick. There were no confiscations that night and I was simply deluged with the stuff. Never was anything more welcome: we never wanted for quinine again at that camp. Later, when, as the men died, I went through their kit – as somebody had to – I found that nearly every man had also secreted a bottle of 500 tablets in his kit-bag – on the principle of one for the camp and one for himself. Other medicines were brought; this was before antibiotics had penetrated to the Far East, but sulphonamides were made and I discovered, I hope rightly, that they had a peculiar bitter flavour by which they could be recognised. On the principle that some treatment is occasionally better than none, I sometimes used sulphonamides identified only by flavour. Nobody suffered.

One of the most remarkable incidents of our whole internment occurred at Ambon. It was, as I have said, a staging-post for the more distant Japanese garrisons on the route back to Java, and one day when the men were at work in the dock, a shipload of badly wounded Japanese officers arrived at the dockside. The idea, our men gathered, was that the Japanese should transfer to another ship, which was standing empty at the other side of the dock. There was no arrangement to transport them across from one ship to the other; presumably the walking wounded were to get themselves across and somehow manhandle those who could not walk; the Japanese were always callous to their wounded, or so it appeared to us.

Our men stood by and watched, and quite suddenly, these same men, starved to near-death, bereft of their friends, beaten, humiliated, submitted to every possible indignity and kept in almost indescribable squalor by the Japanese, could stand the sight of these pathetic wounded no longer. They went on board and carried those Japanese who could not walk, much to their incredulous surprise, between the ships. This says something to me about the boundless compassion of our people – of the ordinary chap – a compassion probably heightened by the suffering they had been through. There was absolutely no thought of revenge in their minds, though I have no doubt that a good many of our people's remarks to the wounded Japanese were, to say the least, pithy.

This experience did our men a great deal of good; it restored their pride, and with it their morale. One of the men put it to me quite simply: 'We couldn't just stand by and let the poor buggers drag themselves across on their stomachs.' When the ordinary chap is down to rock bottom, it does not, as some might suppose, bring out the worst in him: it brings out the best.

7

RETURN TO JAVA

Our stay in Ambon lasted from June to August 1944 and then we were sent back to Java. The 650 of us travelled in two ships, approximately 150 in one and 500, of which I was one, in the other. The smaller party left first. On our small ship (the *Maros Maru*) the holds were, fortunately, already full – with, I think, drums of oil – so we were on the deck and on the hatches, hopelessly overcrowded. Part of the deck was occupied by a woodpile – for cooking purposes – and I started off by living on this. I found it marginally more comfortable than the bare steel deck as, in our emaciated state, contact between one's hip and the deck was very painful at night and prevented sleep. At least, on the woodpile, it was possible to arrange a hip-hole. I came down to deck-level as the wood was used up.

The ship had no radio and the Japanese were obviously conscious that we, 500 of us, outnumbered them by something like 25 to 1, even though they were the ones with the rifles – and that we were only about a thousand miles from the north coast of Australia. A mutiny and a smart turn left would have got us there in a few days, had we been fit and had we been able to organise ourselves – a fact of which we were also well aware. So they took several measures to see that we did not try to seize the ship: they sent an aircraft over us most days, presumably to see that we were on course, but their chief precaution, diabolical in its simplicity, was to see that we were physically incapable of making the effort. Our rations were therefore immediately dropped to starvation-point. We were given rice gruel twice a day – about 60 to 80 grams of rice daily – and nothing else whatsoever except water, and not very much of that.

We were a mixed lot: there were a few who, like myself, had so far kept free from serious infection apart from malaria and were therefore only suffering from plain malnutrition, and there were some who were frankly ill with deficiency symptoms. In between was a group, by far the majority, who had had both dysentery and malaria, had made a partial recovery hindered by dietary deficiencies and were on the edge of serious illness though, at the start of the voyage, free from overt gross deficiency signs. And there were a few fat men – men who for one reason or another had had more than their fair share of white rice, like the carpenter I mentioned before. Apart from these few, we were all pitifully emaciated. It was hard to believe, but we were the group who had been sent by the Japanese from Haruku to Ambon a month or two before as 'fit men.'

Within a day or so, we were reduced to a state where we became quite incapable of organising ourselves sufficiently to take any sort of concerted action, and to add to everyone's troubles, the first ship to leave, with the smaller party, was attacked by Allied aircraft and set on fire. Fortunately, they managed to beach her on a nearby island. Most of the party succeeded in getting ashore, having lost all their belongings. They had a higher proportion of sick than we did and one man behaved outstandingly well in the incident. The ship was burning and was said to be loaded with bombs, but he stayed on board, throwing anything that would float to the men in the water, some of whom he had personally thrown overboard as they were too ill to help themselves. They set up some sort of scratch camp, and when we came past, we picked them up. When I talked to him afterwards, the man who had saved so many made one point very clear: it was true he had stayed on board to get the men off, but he had also noticed that the Japanese guards and the crew were at a meal when the attack occurred. Having seen the men off, when the Japanese had also gone, he went to the crew's quarters and personally finished up their meal before leaving the ship himself. As he said, if he was going to be blown up he might as well be blown up with a full stomach as with an empty one. That was his story, anyway. His name was Mason, he was a builder in peacetime and he was awarded the George Cross for his action. We now had a company of 650, less those few – I cannot now remember how many – who succumbed in the attack. The Dutch doctor, Dr Bryan, from the smaller ship joined me.

We hugged the coastlines of all the islands on our route, some of them mere dots on the map. Many were beautiful, though one missed the lush yellow-greens of more temperate climates. The people all seemed to live by fishing and built their bamboo huts right on the seashore or even over the sea. We often passed frail-looking craft, many with out-riggers, miles from the shore, and once saw a small sailing-ship with a high stern reminiscent of Elizabethan sailing vessels in Europe. This tiny ship was complete with a platform over the stern with holes in it and one of the crew squatting – it made a touching domestic picture.

The *Maros Maru*, an old converted steamship of a few hundred tons, was now powered (if 'powered' is the right word) by a diesel engine, and this was worn out. At no time could we make any reasonable speed and every few days the motor broke down completely. Fortunately, and entirely by chance, we had among us two garage men from Reading who somehow managed to dismantle the engine whenever it broke down and got it going for a few more days. Our journey was to take us two months.

We suffered the starvation diet for 14 days. After about seven days men started dying in large numbers, many from acute beri-beri, which affected the brain (so-called Wernicke's encephalopathy). The men would quite suddenly become euphoric and many sang, rather tunelessly. About a day later, there was slurring of speech, dribbling at the mouth, squinting and awkwardness of movement. The patients remained fairly rational when answering questions but were otherwise (fortunately) in a happy, dreamy state. On the third or fourth day, they became delirious and died. It was a grotesque situation, particularly at night, with several dying men about the deck

96

singing. Some men just died; no special symptoms developed, they just passed away. Some even seemed to decide to die. On several occasions, I saw this, once in a personal friend, who in earlier days had been my batman. He gave up, said he was going to die and, despite my pleadings, was dead in 24 hours. I have heard of this happening in Eastern nations, but not before in Europeans. Obviously, malnutrition was a big factor, but the will entered into it as well. The carpenter who had grown fat on illicit white rice died almost at the beginning of the starvation period without losing any of his fat.

I personally was in a fortunate position in that I had a job of work to do which forced me to keep going, though standing up was an effort. We really had no means whatsoever of treating the sick and dying on board, but at least it was possible to go round and talk to them. The determination necessary to perform even this simple action probably kept me alive at this time.

In this early stage of the voyage, men were dying at the rate of 15 or more a day. We did our best to give them some sort of sea burial but were too weak to do much more than heave the bodies over the side with a few words from the prayer-book – the prayer-book given to me by Clifford Martin when he married Emmie and me. So often were we stopped with engine trouble that we frequently stayed in the same place for 24 hours or more. The situation then became gruesome because we had no means of weighting the bodies down, and after about 12 hours in the warm tropical sea, if the water was calm and we were near the shore, they would float up to the surface all around us. Sometimes there would be as many as six, bloated but unfortunately often still recognisable. Some of the stronger among us tried swimming to them and slitting them with a knife to make them go down. Fish finally finished the job.

I felt it my duty to go through the kit of the dead, though most did not have much. Obviously, somebody had to do this; it could not just lie around, and sometimes contained things useful to the living. I usually did it in the presence of the dead man's friends, and if there was anything useful, they were generally the recipients. It was better for me to do it than to leave it to the friends; they felt better about it because, in a sense, it became official – and any small trinkets, any mementoes of the dead man's wife, could be handed over to them. It was at this time that I found the bottles of quinine that most of the men carried. Men were by now dying so fast that even the Japanese on board became alarmed and, from one of the islands we passed on the way, brought the carcase of a cow on board. It stank when it arrived; by the time it was cut up, it stank even more, and finally it had to go overboard. I do not now remember whether we were given any or not, but it would have been quite inedible.

So we made our slow, grotesque way to Makasar in Sulawesi (The Celebes). In the harbour there, local workmen came on board to try to repair the ship's engine. By now I realised that without more food I should soon die and decided that the time had come to swop my watch. I approached one of the native workmen – clandestinely, as the Japanese wanted watches – and in Malay and sign langauge, made a deal with him. I would give him my watch if he would next day bring me ducks (cooked), eggs, peanuts, chillies and sugar. I gave him the watch and waited until next day. He was as good as his word. He kept his bargain, this unknown inhabitant of Makasar. He brought me two cooked ducks, several dozen eggs, pounds of peanuts, many chillies and some sugar. And, equally important, managed to hand them over to me without the Japanese seeing. I gave half to my friends and retired to my woodpile with the other half. Obviously, the duck, already cooked, had to be eaten straight away – that was enough for the first day. The eggs had to be eaten raw as there was no means of cooking them: all had beating hearts, but the embryos were minute. I found that a good way to eat raw eggs was to grind up some chillies in a mug, break an egg over them and mix it all up well to make a fiery yellow sauce and then break another egg into it without damaging the yolk. This was drunk down in a single gulp – a sort of poor man's prairie oyster. It may seem revolting, but we were near death from starvation and it was, in those circumstances, a glorious

98

gastronomic experience. The rest of the food was spread over several days. It was really a marvellous bargain and undoubtedly saved my life. Little did Messrs Camerer Cuss and Co. Ltd., in New Oxford Street, know, when they sold this watch to me (a present from my aunt Annie) in 1938 for £3 15s (£3.75) that it would save my life six years later. It also kept very good time.

Men were still dying as fast as ever as we lay in Makasar harbour, and whereas leaving bodies floating behind us in uninhabited places was dreadful enough, to be surrounded by them in harbour, with other ships around us, was the ultimate obscenity. I personally felt ashamed that this should happen and we could do nothing about it. It made the whole situation doubly horrible.

A few mangoes came aboard at Makasar, the first fresh fruit that we had seen for many a day. We found that they played havoc with our lips, making them quite raw, but they were good. We had seen very little scurvy, which is due to lack of fresh fruit or vegetables or fresh meat. I had, in fact, diagnosed it once, possibly correctly (I had never seen it before) in a Dutch soldier on board this ship. After Makasar, the rations improved a little; we were given fish-head and seaweed soup (much nicer than it sounds) with our rice, the ration of which was somewhat better. Sea cucumber – a slug-like animal also called a sea slug – was also served in the soup. This was, one must admit, rather an acquired taste, but it was food.

That journey was no place for humour but one incident sticks in the mind. We all had body lice – lice are no respecters of persons, British or Dutch, officers or other ranks. All of us had some sort of covering and they lurked in the seams. The only way that we had to deal with them was to pick them off by hand, and the convention was that you squashed each one between the thumb and forefinger before throwing it away. One Dutch officer, his pride and dignity still more intact than most people's declined to do this: he simply picked them off and threw them down disdainfully, still crawling, spared to infest the next man. This was the only time that we came near to an international misunderstanding.

99

One incident on this voyage I personally regret very much, though I felt it was unavoidable, and events proved me right. The journal that I had kept throughout our imprisonment had now reached 600 pages. I was much too far gone to do much about this on board the ship but I still had a pencil and was trying to keep a list of the names of the dead. I was seen one day doing this by a Japanese, who got into a rage and told me I was not to write and that anything I did write would be taken from me when we came to Java, where they were looking for paper – by which he obviously meant that they were looking for writing. It struck me that there could be only two reasons for this: either they were anxious to obliterate any record of conduct that even they considered shameful, or worse, they were on the lookout for anything which could be distorted to form propaganda – to give, in fact, a favourable account of life in a POW camp.

(I met examples of this after I came home, so this, it turned out, was a strong possibility. Emmie had in her possession a newspaper cutting reporting an interview with an officer prisoner in one of the Japanese camps in Java giving a very rosy – and quite false – picture of the life we were leading. I still have it. It suggests to me that there was coercion, and one can only pity the officer forced to write it.)

My journal was a very personal message to Emmie rather than a historical document and I did not want it to get into the wrong hands. Moreover, dreadful thought, had any part of it been distorted to use for propaganda, I could guess who they might ask to broadcast it. I felt that I might still have a usefulness as a doctor, and anyway did not much relish this. Had I refused, I should clearly have been put to death, and the journal was not worth this. So I turned the matter over in my mind for a long time, took out a few paintings of Haruku, secreted them between the layers of my pack and sank the rest of the book in the Java sea.

We arrived in Java in October after some 60 days at sea. We had covered 1,200 miles as the crow flies, but in reality travelled far further as we hugged the coastlines. Considerably more than half the company died during this voyage and most of the rest of us were in a very poor way. There were times when standing up required a considerable effort.

In our poor physical state, keeping records was extremely difficult or impossible and we had to rely on memory. My energies, such as they were, had to be directed to the sick. One was intimately involved in a personal relationship with the sick and dying; we had grown to be friends during the time we were together, from Semarang onwards. This even touched on the keeping of records – one was no dispassionate observer. At the end of the voyage I concluded that 307 British had died. The Dutch numbers were kept by the Dutch officers.

* * *

Note (added in 1983): A Dutch book has been published on the whole POW experience in the Moluccas and Flores: J H W Veenstra, *Als Krijgsgevangene naar de Molukken en Flores* Martinus Nijohoff, s' – Gravenhage, 1982. There the figure of 308 British deaths and 63 Dutch is given for this voyage. This discrepancy of one in the number of British deaths is hardly surprising in view of the circumstances. So, out of the total of 650 men (British and Dutch), the deaths totalled 370 or 371. The Dutch figure is probably more likely to be right as they could come back to the problem after the war; we moved on.

In addition, the book gives the deaths due to the sinking by Allied action in 1943 of the unmarked ship, the *Suez Maru*, taking POWs from Haruku to Java (the party of sick that left Haruku in September 1943, numbering 650). These figures are worse than I feared when I wrote the account (see p. 58). Those drowned numbered 539 (412 British and 127 Dutch). (I am grateful to Professor Audus for translating from the Dutch for me.)

If this figure of 539 is added to the deaths on Haruku island (415) and the deaths on the recent journey, the total is 1,325 among the 2,075 who came on this ghastly expedition, leaving 750 survivors, a number of whom were too ill to go on much longer. (Or 1,324 deaths and 751 survivors if my figures are used.)

8

JAVA TO SINGAPORE

On arrival in Java we were searched as I had been warned and finished up in a camp outside Jakarta (Batavia). There we rejoined those of our people who had not come on the Ambon working party with us and had therefore missed the dreadful journey on the *Maros Maru*, so I met Clifford Beales, Alastair Forbes and Leslie Audus again.

The first evening we were there, Dr Bryan and I, the two doctors who had been on the disastrous journey, were sent for by the Japanese Commandant of the camp. We were made to stand at the bottom of a flight of stone steps and, after keeping us waiting for a proper time, he came out and stood with an interpreter at the top. This procedure was common, almost universal, when Japanese officers were addressing us: very sensitive to their small stature, and always concerned with loss of face, they preferred to address us from a height. The officer, through his interpreter, made a speech to us. We had just come on a journey during which more than half the prisoners had died, he said. This was our fault. We were doctors and our duty was to keep the men alive, not to kill them. The Nippon Government was very worried that so many prisoners were dying, because the International Red Cross (the first time I had ever heard a Japanese use this term) was asking questions about why so many prisoners died in their camps. He knew why the men had died. We had killed them by being bad doctors. We were murderers (long pause). We would be required to go to the Japanese headquarters next day to sign a paper to say that we had murdered the men so that the Red

102

Cross would know. We were then dismissed.

Fantastic as this speech may seem, we had become used to apparent fantasy and this was a no more unreal situation than many we had been through. We already knew, from several years' experience, that it was common for the Japanese to make this sort of threat to see how we reacted, so we simply stared straight ahead, not apparently reacting at all. For all I knew, they thought we would believe what they said, and would be suitably chastened, in which case, of course, they would not have lost face. I personally gave the matter a little careful thought and decided that, if forced to sign such a document I would so do, but my name would be F Undercoercion Philps.

They did not send for us to sign the paper, but they had, of course, given us a vital piece of information. They would not have been unduly upset by the attitude of the Red Cross if they had still regarded themselves – even after pulling out of Ambon – as masters of the Far Eastern situation. We knew, in that moment, that not only had they lost the war, but they knew it. I think they never gave us credit for this sort of reasoning, so they probably did not suspect that they had given anything away. it must be admitted, of course, that officers in charge of POW camps were probably not very bright or they would have been in jobs requiring more intellectual capacity. Anyway, this made the day of our return to Java – in late October 1944 – a red-letter day. We did not expect, as I have said, to survive to the end, but it was good to know that the Japanese knew they were beaten – and any nation capable of the treachery of Pearl Harbour richly deserved it.

The rations at the Jakarta camp were rather better than we had experienced for a long time, ever since Semarang; the cooks even ground a sort of flour and made coarse bread. One was able to pick up some of the strength lost on the journey, which was a good thing, so far as I was concerned, in view of what was to follow. Two other things about this camp stand out in my mind. The first was that I had scabies (an infestation by a mite that lives in the skin, causing great irritation) and the second that the lute had turned up again. My scabies was treated by the only method we had which was effective: you made a mixture of powdered sulphur and coconut oil and covered yourself with it, literally from head to toe, then spent the whole day out of doors, wearing no clothes at all. It was better to stay in the shade as acute sunburn of the bits – not much, it is true – that had not become tanned because of the dictates of decency would have been most painful. It was not really a comfortable day in any case, because everything one touched or sat on became oily, but it was nice to be rid of the itch. To complete the treatment, we had to boil our clothing and bedclothes – such as we had. In the comparative luxury of Jakarta we could also delouse ourselves.

It was good to see the lovely lute again, the lute that had come into my possession at the hospital at Semarang but which did not come to Haruku with us – perhaps fortunately, because it would not have survived the journey there. It was so light to carry about that somebody had always managed to get it from camp to camp, and here it was again, strung as a guitar, with any wire that came to hand. There was one man with considerable skill as a musician and we derived enormous pleasure from it. I even practised it a little myself and could just about pick out a tune. The lute had a great advantage: a beginner could practise so quietly that others in the same hut were not troubled. I have often wondered about the earlier (and later) history of this beautiful instrument. I hope it survives.

I was relieved of medical duties for the short time I was in this camp. I had been continuously on duty for two and a half years and there were others to run the medical service there – and having not too bad a time, considering everything. Looking back, my short stay was an oasis of relief and rest, with time to sit and talk – and new people to talk to. But it was not to last; the time came for me to move on again and I began to feel like the Flying Dutchman, but I knew the men, they knew me, and by this time our destinies had become so interwoven that one did not wish to drop out if they were to be moved on. It was rumoured that we were to go to a railway in Burma – later to become notorious when the facts were

104

revealed, but we knew nothing of this at the time. It was pretty clear that none of us would survive a third working party, but we had little say in this and we were sure that we had to die soon, one way or another. I was, as far as I know, the only doctor who had been with two working camps already, Semarang and Haruku (three, if you count Ambon) and I emphasise that I made no personal choice to go on yet another working party. I hope that the men had chosen me because, though many of them from our recent journey had to remain at Jakarta as they were too ill to go on, some were in this new working party. There was something very important about being among men I liked and who, I hoped, liked me. If we were to die, we might as well die among friends. Rudi Springer, beloved of the Haruku men, was also in the party.

I had managed to regain some strength at Jakarta, though we were all still quite emaciated. Once again, I was impressed by the physical toughness of those born skinny. During one of our darkest times I was chatting with one of the men in the party and he described how, as one of 12 children of a farm labourer somewhere in Gloucestershire (what a ring these names had – pure nostalgia in those times), their midday meal was always bread and lard. So many were they, and so small their cottage, that they could not all sit down to a meal, so they were lined up in the lane outside. He was always a skinny man, and though I do not know his final fate, at that time he was managing to cope better than many.

We set off from Jakarta, heading north. Our journey was less uncomfortable than our previous ones; we were on deck, not overcrowded, and our rations contained fish-head and seaweed soup with sea slugs (the last still not a very well acquired taste), so we managed to keep body and soul together. I imagined that we were heading for Rangoon but in fact we arrived in Singapore. We were told the ship that was to have taken us on the rest of our journey had been sunk by a torpedo. So there seemed a chance that we would not go to the Burma–Thailand railway after all.

We were billeted in a small camp in Singapore, and our working party was on general duty in the docks, with a good deal of tidying up after Allied bombing attacks. As we had just arrived and had left our seriously ill men in Java, there was nobody needing in-patient care, and I had what was for me a rare treat: I went with the outside working party to the docks as a supernumerary medical orderly.

I must confess to mixed feelings when herded into an open lorry and driven through Singapore. How far we had fallen from Imperial splendour and how shameful was our present condition. The local inhabitants of Singapore had, I felt, a right to expect us to defend them successfully. They had not asked us there in the first place and the least they could expect was protection. In this, we had failed: why we had failed was of no account: we had failed.

My other feeling, which to some extent offset the first, was pride in British motor-car technology. Nearly all the cars in the streets were British – those left behind when the civilians left Singapore. Obviously, the only people in cars were the Japanese and those working for them, and the Japanese were using the more prestigious ones, mainly large Wolseleys and Austins. These had probably not been serviced – knowing the Japanese – since the fall of the island well over two years before and they were still going well.

One day when we were out at the docks, we had a remarkable piece of luck. A bomb had hit Singapore Cold Store on the dockside and made a large hole in its roof, allowing the cold rooms to warm up. Their contents were obviously going to rot if left in the store – much was decomposing already – so everyone went in and helped himself to the largest chunk of still-frozen meat or fish he could carry. The problem was to cook our loot: we had obviously taken far more than we could possibly eat before it went bad and it was essential that we should cook as much as we could on the spot. The only container we had was our tea-boiler – a fairly large iron vessel heated over a wood fire. We were already brewing tea in it so we put as many lumps of meat as it would hold into the tea, stoked up the fire and waited for the urn to boil up. We had only a limited time before we had to leave the docks, so we boiled it for as long as we could, and when we could wait no longer, we took the pieces out, cut them up and ate them. I shall never forget the sensation of eating meat – best-quality beef – that was boiled white for a thin layer on the outside, red and uncooked for an equally thin layer beneath and all the inside part crunching with ice crystals when you bit it. The whole was covered with tealeaves. Such considerations did not worry us unduly: it was a good day. We managed to carry most of our haul back to the camp. I do not remember the Japanese making a fuss and have no doubt that they saw to it that they got an ample share.

Another thing that I discovered on the Singapore dockside was the usefulness of copra. Copra is dried coconut roughly cut up into large pieces and is a source of oil, normally used for soap and, presumably, margarine. Infested with rats, mice and their attendant stray cats, whole warehouses were full of it and we found it most valuable, for not only was it a source of oil when chewed but it made a satisfactory – if rather smelly – springy bed. There are few other things that you can both eat and lie on and I spent several comfortable afternoons – in my capacity as supernumerary medical orderly – dozing on the copra.

Singapore harbour was used as a refuelling base by such German U-boats as found their way into those waters. One morning we were at the dock when one came in. The crew disembarked, and no doubt because their commander saw us, he determined upon a smart parade, so they marched up the dockside. We seized the opportunity to whistle in unison (I now forget what tune) out of time with their step and went on until they broke step. A small matter, but it gave us considerable pleasure. The Germans, no doubt, were in a quandary. I am sure they felt embarrassed in front of us with the Japanese as their allies – they probably felt as we did about our captors and had a certain sympathy for us. Ours were the only European faces they would see at that time in the Far East.

We were soon moved to another small camp in Singapore. All the huts were of bamboo and palm-leaf *atap*; the beds were also of bamboo, and they had been occupied by local labourers for a long time before we arrived. Bamboo is the

107

bedbug's ideal habitat – old bamboo with cracks in it, enabling them to get into the cavities and set up home in great comfort and safety. These huts were simply crawling with them.

Some people can be bitten by bedbugs and hardly notice; others are horribly irritated by a single bite. I am one of the second sort. Each morning there were dozens of them in the corners of my mosquito net and I spent an unpleasant ten minutes squashing them all – a process that makes a most objectionable smell reminiscent of bitter almonds – and by the next morning there would be just as many again. An iron bedstead can be disinfested by playing a blowlamp on the tubing, but our beds were of bamboo, so this was hardly a practical solution and it was clear to me that there was no way of disinfecting the huts, short of burning them down.

I was being kept awake night after night by the bugs biting me, which might not seem very important had it not been for the fact that I had to do my best to provide a medical service for the camp, along with my Dutch colleagues. The matter became quite serious, so I decided that I must try to get a night's sleep a week, bedbugs or no, in order to carry on. Though I do not now remember how I got them, I had come by a large number of 'Tubunic' ampoules of morphine of the type issued to aircrew, corroded and hopelessly out of date, and decided that once a week I should dope myself with one of the ampoules by drinking the contents. I chose Thursday night, probably for no better reason than that I had the idea on a Thursday and felt that by doing this only one night a week I should not become addicted. (Though I have several times said that we expected to die, this fact – that I wished not to become addicted to morphine – suggests to me now that I retained a measure of hope.) The scheme worked very well: the bugs bit me to their hearts' content on Thursday nights without waking me and I got enough sleep to last the week, however much they disturbed me on other nights. I had managed to keep a toothbrush and found that the bugs even lurked in the bristles. The flavour was not nice if one was sufficiently unwary to forget to turn them out before brushing the teeth.

We had managed to steal some drums of palm oil, a brilliant orange, opaque, thick, greasy oil normally used in soap manufacture. We found it could be eaten with a spoon – though it played havoc with the spoon if you left it in overnight, turning it bright green. it was not unpleasant, provided that you limited yourself to a couple of tablespoonfuls a day, but it tinged the skin yellow, making us look as though we had a mild attack of jaundice.

At this camp I caught dysentery – a bacillary dysentery – in the most ridiculous way. our rice ration was brought ready cooked to our quarters by two carriers and clearly one of them had helped himself by dipping his hand in . He was suffering from dysentery and infected several of us on that day. It is an ironic thought that I had come through Haruku, where infection was all around me, had personally looked after many hundreds of patients with the disease, had performed many pathological investigations on infected material and had worked out a method of dysentery-proof living that served me well for a year, and now should be infected in this way, through the negligence of a food-carrier who failed to wash his hands before stealing my rations. My Dutch colleagues gave me great care, and I recovered – indeed, it was quite pleasant to have somebody else care for me at last – but I was, like everybody else, much weakened by the infection. We were given the news by the Japanese at this time, in April 1945, of the death of President Roosevelt, and I remember being too flat on my back to be able to stand up to do him honour.

A small contribution to my recovery was our receipt, in May, of half a Red Cross parcel each. This was our first acquaintance with them, and the announcement of their arrival caused enormous excitement. They had come to Singapore a year or more before and had been stored in one of the warehouses. When they were delivered to us, it turned out that they were parcels packed for Europe, so none of the wrappings were especially designed for the tropics. This did not, of course, affect the tinned foods (if they were intact and unrusted, which some were not) but the chocolate had to be seen to be believed. It was a white, crumbling slab of amorphous

109

material no longer retained by its silver paper, having oozed out all round, and through holes in the paper when it melted in the heat, before it finally dried out. Nevertheless, picking out fragments of the wrapping paper as we went, we ate it and suffered no ill-effects. If only Mr Cadbury could have seen us then: I was forcefully reminded of the slip of paper he included with his chocolate in peacetime, promising to refund cost and postage if the product was not in perfect condition.

There was condensed milk in the parcels; some of the tins had been punctured and the contents had oozed out and solidified. The protein content of milk is such that this might have led to the growth of harmful bacteria in the tins, but I felt that the amount of sugar added to the milk in its manufacture was probably sufficient to inhibit such growth and told the men to get on and eat it – they needed it so badly. Fortunately, I was right. Moreover, the flavour of the milk still in the tin was unaffected by the possible entry of air. Tinned tomatoes and Mother somebody's Irish stew were the other contents. The tomatoes were welcome, unremarkable, and mostly water, but oh, that stew! For three years we had had rice, vegetables, some meat, some fish, sometimes some chillies and the occasional onion: the impact of the flavour of Irish stew was such that every ingredient could be tasted separately. It was a truly remarkable experience. Quite memorable.

It was at about this time that I realised I had pulmonary tuberculosis. I had been feeling rotten since having dysentery, getting the shivers in the evenings. When I noticed a continuous bubbling sensation near the apex of my right lung with a local area of pleurisy, the diagnosis was obvious. By now I was finding difficulty in standing up without feeling dizzy and could not do my job, so this seemed to be the point at which I would depart. And then, an event occurred which was life-saving for me: we were moved to Changi Gaol, wonderful Changi Gaol, civilised and, by our standards, luxurious. It had houses made of brick, mains electricity, even cultural activities going on. It also had a garden, frogs and money-lenders.

9

CHANGI GAOL

Though it had not been ever thus, the great virtue of Changi Gaol when we arrived was that, apart from its good buildings, it had a rare person indeed, a reasonable Japanese officer, in command. The basic rations of the prisoners were, as everywhere else, in short supply, but the Commandant allowed the prisoners to cultivate as much space for gardens as they required, so the vegetable ration was more or less unlimited. Moreover, some of the prisoners had been planters (rubber growers mostly) from Malaya who knew about the local crops and how to grow them. These factors, the good buildings and the rations above starvation level, had enabled a stable community to develop. We only came into it late, for the last three months as it turned out, so we came into the community in its fully developed state. It had an adequate medical service – people were even writing medical papers and studying for their MRCP examination – and it had good cooking facilities.

The camp cooks worked with some imagination: they invented the 'doover' – a sort of rissole made from the meat ration, some vegetables and seasoning and fried in oil. These came on the menu twice a week and were a change from anything we had had in the last three years. The name derived from hors d'oeuvres, some serviceman exclaiming when first presented with one, 'This is like horse doovers', and it stuck. There was an abundance of electric cooking rings at Changi, repaired with scrounged electric wire whenever they broke down, for any man who had a little private food to cook. How the circuits stood the enormous load without setting the place on fire I shall never know. With all these advantages, those who had

111

been at the gaol some time were reasonably well-covered; the only emaciated people were the late arrivals like ourselves.

A small amount of rice was set aside to supplement the ration of those who were wasted to near-death. I was not now officially on duty, but Rudi Springer and I felt that we should decide who, among our own men, most needed the extra food. (We could now safely give the men extra white rice because there were sufficient vegetables to prevent them developing beriberi.) It was always important that any allocation of this sort among a mixed British and Dutch community should be made, if humanly possible, by a committee of two doctors, one of each nationality. In this way we avoided any ill-informed criticism or complaint of unfairness – a small but vital point. So we invented the Springer–Philps test of emacia-tion – a test as objective as we could make it. Objectivity was essential for our own peace of mind; it was not that either of us would have given extra rations to anybody we particularly favoured – rather the opposite. Just as Springer had said at Haruku, referring to a particular man: 'I dislike that man so much that I am most careful to give him the best treatment I can', so in this situation, one would be inclined, if one disliked a man, to give him extra rations more easily so as to be quite sure in one's mind that there was no bias against him. An objective test avoided this kind of reversed unfairness.

The test itself was not difficult to perform. The men who were possible candidates for extra food were asked to strip completely and walk past us. We sat, viewing them from the side, our eyes level with their hips. It is important for me to explain that all the men in our recently arrived party were little more than skeletons covered by a thin layer of muscle and skin. A fatty layer was virtually non-existent. The but-tocks were our concern: they are normally composed of fat and muscle and are a good indication of the amount of wasting. If the bulge of the buttocks has disappeared com-pletely, that man has little reserve left; this was the basis of our test. The sacrum is a bone at the bottom of the spine and is normally quite invisible from the side because of the but-tocks. If one looks at a skeleton from the side, the whole

112

length of the sacrum is visible, so, as each man walked slowly past us, we looked to see if we could see the whole length of his sacrum from the side. If we could, he was given the extra ration. This, in well-fed peacetime, may seem almost unbelievable, but it was a very good test: it picked out those men who really could not go on without a little extra, but as rice was in short supply, did not let through the net anybody who could still manage. The number of men we picked out in this way neatly balanced the amount of rice we had available for extra rations.

By now I was in a pretty poor state and was put on garden duties. This was a post reserved for an officer in a fairly advanced state of emaciation and was rather reminiscent of the Chiltern Hundreds: he and several sick men could be said to be doing a job but in reality were able to sit in the shade, in the very pleasant surroundings of the garden, and have an enormous midday meal of vegetable stew. The actual garden supervision was done by experts, the planters from up-country who had a great knowledge of local plants and their cultivation. The men who worked there did so willingly, because of the excellent midday meal. The whole arrangement was gentle and amicable, a change from the hectic, tense life in a Japanese working camp.

Despite the improvement in my circumstances, it was clear to me that if I was to survive – and having got this far, I badly wanted to survive – I must devise a way of getting some extra animal protein. The solution was really quite easy: tapioca flour and coconut oil were available (I forget now how I obtained them) and I had a cooking pan. I had noticed that on some mornings the ditches round the camp fairly resounded with the croaking of frogs, so I made a small net with some wire and a piece of cloth, listened when I woke up, and if it was a good day for frogs, went out and caught about 20, killed them as kindly as I could – I even apologised to them, explaining that it was either them or me – saved their backs, arms and legs and took my catch home. There I prepared a pastry of tapioca flour, water, coconut oil and salt, lined my pan with it, added the frog bits, some salt, an onion and some

113

chillies if I had them, put in some water, put on a crust of the same pastry, engraved my name on it and there was a frog pie for lunch.

Some ingenious engineer in the camp had designed a cooking stove which ran on the only fuel abundant at that time – old car-sump oil. This was lit several times a week for private cooking and was invaluable, even though it showered the whole of the area with smuts and played havoc with our washing. Into this stove in the morning went my frog pie, to be ready, piping hot, at lunch-time. It was pretty good – better, I must admit, if one forgot it was made of frogs; difficult when there were some 40 frogs' legs (and another 40 frogs' arms) in it – and it undoubtedly helped to keep me alive as I could make one quite often, depending on the supply of frogs and the availability of the oven. Those frogs died in a good cause.

Even with the frog pies I was making no real headway so I had to try more drastic measures, if only to keep the tuberculosis under control until possible release. There was money available in Changi Gaol, possibly a considerable amount of money. It had been a POW camp for years when we arrived and therefore we, as strangers, were in a position to see it rather more clearly than those who had become used to its ways. No doubt it had had its good and bad times, but when we came there it was, in a sense, a microcosm of a city: it had admirable medical and dental services, it had cooks who showed great initiative, it had experts looking after the garden, it had craftsmen and technicians, and, amazingly, it had businessmen – moneylenders. These men are my present concern.

Several POWs whose minds worked in this way had started off in business by selling a ring (or watch, but by now these were scarce) outside the camp for dollars. (The Singapore dollar was valued at the time of the Japanese invasion at 2 s 3 d, which is just 11p. After the Japanese took over, it would have been difficult to value because they were printing dollar notes without numbers on them and the Chinese, ever good counterfeiters, were taking advantage of this by printing more for themselves.) These men thus established a contact and other people sold their rings through them, so they became agents and presumably made a profit on each sale. Gradually, they became wealthy – one supposes, very wealthy – in Japanese (or Chinese) printed unnumbered Singapore dollars. They then had the problem that, in ordinary times, their money would be quite worthless – it only had a value in this artificial situation – so they devised a method of turning it into real currency.

Money was needed by the other prisoners to buy extra food and, in some cases, tobacco, and the businessmen made it known that they would exchange their dud dollars for pounds sterling. They would, in fact, accept undated cheques drawn on British banks, to be dated later, and pay dollars for them, intending to change them after release, provided they considered the man giving them the cheque to be a 'good risk'. A cheque, of course, can be written on anything, provided that it contains the necessary information. So these men were paying out dollars in exchange for cheques promising to pay them in pounds sterling, the rate of exchange decided by themselves. Whatever one feels about this conduct, it did enable me to give a cheque for £50 and receive in exchange 110 dollars, worth, in fact, a few pence each. In case I should die before the cheque could be cashed (or I should stop it), my man required a separate, witnessed agreement, which I still have. I notice that it is No. 36, so 35 people before me had entered into deals. It is dated 7 July 1945, so there were still several weeks to go, and I have no doubt he did good business in that time. He might even have been sorry to see the end of the war.

Money lenders agreement.

I had considerable unease about making this deal, simply because I was regarded by any man as a good risk, likely to have £50 in the bank, but the rank and file, probably poor risks, would probably not have been able to use this facility. It seemed unfair – we on the working parties had stopped thinking like this – but death appeared the alternative, even if the war finished soon. I well remember, when the deal took place, my man telling me of the great risk he was taking of never getting the cheque home, so he was sorry – 'old boy' – that he could not give a better rate of exchange.

I spent my 110 dollars on food – protein food, eggs and fish – which could be bought from the local population. The fish were remarkable: small and sprat-like, they appeared to have been buried for some time. They stank to High Heaven, particulary when being cooked, but fried and mixed with rice they tasted very good – one only has to think of ripe Stilton to have a comparison.

My cheque was paid in soon after we arrived home. Though the 110 dollars I got from the deal were contributory to saving my life, I still find this a disturbing tale, perhaps best read in conjunction with the Ambon incident, when simpler men than these showed compassion to the Japanese wounded.

The cultural activities that went on a Changi were many, and at least one person put in a great deal of practice drawing for the camp magazine; Ronald Searle possibly developed his highly individual style there. Clever people had made several radios, about which others have already written, which were most ingeniously hidden and operated so that they were never discovered – and we knew the news every day. The most effective one was built inside the hollowed-out wooden rafter that formed part of a bed-frame so that no part of it was visible from the outside. The electric current to work it was led in by sticking two wires through fake worm-holes in the wood, which effectively switched it on, and the man who operated it listened with a stethoscope applied to the wood just over the headphone, which was inside the cavity. Possessing a working radio was, the Japanese made clear, punishable by death, so absolute secrecy was essential; even the other prisoners in the

116

operator's hut did not know of its existence. It was worked by only one person and always with his mosquito-net down.

A difficulty arose because the Japanese turned the electricity off at the mains at night and the best news bulletins came through then, so some means had to be devised of making them leave the current on in this particular hut. Fortunately, the end of the hut was close to – and visible from – the guard-room, so a skilled mechanic among the prisoners made the guards an electric clock and fixed it to the wall where they could see it. They had to leave the current on at night if they were to know the time, and it was a matter of no difficulty to lead the wire, secretly, from the clock circuit to the radio.

The news was memorised by the operator, not written, and was then told to four trusted people. These four were the only ones who knew the source of it. The four each told several more, who went into each hut quietly telling everybody. The service achieved great accuracy, the 'memory men' training themselves to recall every detail. We knew exactly what was going on much more quickly than our guards – and much more accurately. So good was the secrecy that none of us knew the source of the bulletins.

There were other radios, one behind a sink which had been made to slide out of the wall, and one in a broomhead, the handle of which had to be leant against an electricity socket to plug it in. We ordinary people only knew all this when were shown it after the Japanese capitulation. The men who oper-ated the radios and those who disseminated the news showed great courage; the Japanese Secret Police, the Kempetai, possi-bly the nastiest in the world, were very active – and much feared – in Singapore, and one shudders to think of the fate of any of these operators had they been caught: death, which they knew they had to expect, would have been a release. It was not until we reached Changi that we knew of the invasion of Europe – and of the Allied victory. We had heard rumours before but with no confirmation.

Because of the news service, we knew about the atomic bombs on Hiroshima and Nagasaki at the same time as the rest of the world and before the Japanese guards – we had to

117

be very careful not to show that we knew – and then we heard the news of the Japanese capitulation. By this time, we were so drained of emotion that it was hardly possible even to raise a cheer or much of a comment. All passion was spent. The waste of life – of the young virile men who had been with us – became our dominant thought.

The moment the Japanese had capitulated, our people fitted up loudspeakers throughout the camp and all news was broadcast. We learned how dietary experts were to be flown to us to advise on the weaning process we would need to get us back to European food. All that actually happened was that we were given half a pound of butter each, which we promptly ate with spoons and were sick for days. We had other supplies dropped to us by parachute, and we had the extraordinary experience of having the whole Japanese guard jump to attention, shout, salute and sit down again whenever one of our officers passed the guardroom – we quite shamelessly took advantage and had them jumping up and down continually for the first day. We had a visit from a party of journalists which included a beautiful New Zealand girl, a strange experience after not seeing a white woman for three and a half years and perhaps a little unfair: we felt unwashed and conscious that we must have smelled rather strange – or so we thought. We learned that Admiral Tojo, Japanese Chief of Staff, had attempted suicide, failed, and was being treated with a substance we had never heard of called penicillin. We had a visit from Lord and Lady Mountbatten.

One incident of this time stands out in my mind. As I said earlier, all the officers had been paid, but only been allowed to retain a minute proportion of our pay, the rest being paid into the 'Japanese Bank' by our captors. After the capitulation, a senior Japanese officer came to the camp and several lorries were driven in, all laden with unnumbered Japanese dollar notes. The Senior British Officer was called and told that this was our money and that he was to distribute it to us. He refused, pointing out that it was quite worthless and insisted that it be taken away again. The Japanese officer, five foot nothing, who had learned his English, it appeared, from the soldiery, stood up, raised himself to his full height and in a final gesture of great dignity said: 'You will not tell me to stuff my money up my jumper' (except that he did not say 'jumper': it is just that I do not want this narrative to become too impolite). Our Senior Officer, with nothing short of a stroke of genius, ordered two accounts officers among the prisoners to go home on the first plane back to Britain and report that we had refused the return of the worthless Japanese money. His prompt action resulted in us all having our back pay as a lump sum in our accounts by the time we arrived home.

I had recovered to some extent from my malnutrition. I now weighed 94 pounds and managed, even though I knew I had tuberculosis, to avoid going home in a ship for the sick – one never knows where that sort of thing might lead. In fact, it led those with tuberculosis to a long sojourn in South Africa. The journey to the dock – the start of the journey home – was perhaps the most terrifying part of the whole three and a half years. We were a party of four, and were taken, with what remained of our kit, from Changi to the harbour in a Jeep. The driver was either mad or showing off and he took us at well over 60 mph on the dirt road. I, and perhaps the others, thought how ironical it would be if, after having lived through that lot, we should end our lives scattered on the road by a madman driver. We survived, but it remains in my mind as one of the most frightening moments of my life.

10

RETURN TO LIFE

We sailed from Singapore, called at Colombo, where we were shown the town by the prettiest Wrens in their prettiest clothes, and left for home. We had seven ex-POW medical officers on board, of whom I was marginally the most senior. Just out of Colombo I was sent for by the ship's MO, who told me that South-East Asia Command (SEAC) had sent him a signal ordering us to examine all of the more than a thousand men on the ship and grade them medically before we arrived at Liverpool. For the first time in my life, I disobeyed an order. I told the medical officer that I did not think any of the medical staff were physically capable of doing this. Whoever gave the order can have had no idea of how we had been living for the past three and a half years. We were simply not fit, we were exhausted, and I felt quite unable to order my colleagues to do this. To my great surprise I heard no more, so some days later I asked the MO what had happened; in fact, why I was not under arrest. He told me that he had informed the Chief MO at SEAC that I was mentally abnormal as a result of my imprisonment, and offered me a drink. The men were not examined and nobody suffered in any way.

* * *

We sailed into Liverpool. Emmie, I hoped, was at Radlett with my mother. I had managed to write her several letters and, from Port Said, to cable the local greengrocer (Hill's in Watling Street, where, as a child, I used to be given overripe

120

plums) to send her and Mother some flowers on account. When we arrived, we were all given a mass X-ray and I was not surprised to be recalled for further pictures as I had already made the diagnosis months ago – and I was shivering in the evenings. The X-ray revealed that I did, in fact, have a fairly extensive shadow in my right lung and I was given what I consider to be the most negligent advice I have ever received. I was told: 'This will need treatment, old boy, but go home for six weeks' leave and then come back and we will arrange it' – no thought at all that I might be infective, no thought that I could, for all they knew, be going back to a house with children in it.

On the train to London I nipped out at a major station, I cannot now remember which, as soon as we stopped there, rushed to the nearest telephone box, phoned Emmie, arranged to meet her at Paddington, got back into the train just as it moved off and met her at a spot on the platform that has become hallowed ground ever since.

Emmie, who had first been a matron at a boys' school and then, for the greater part of the time I was away, cook at a girls' school, weathered the war totally confident that I had survived – though her only concrete information was the Air Ministry notification of August 1943 that I was a prisoner and my postcard of Christmas 1942, which also arrived in August 1943. After that, she had no news until I cabled her from Colombo on my way home in 1945, several weeks after the Japanese capitulation, after a cruelly long delay. We had not been near Singapore town, so could not cable from there, there were no cable facilities in the camp and no notification had reached her.

Next morning I reported myself sick at Shenley Hospital – normally a mental hospital, but taken over by the Services. Laboratory tests did not take long to indicate that I was in a highly infectious state; I was admitted at once. I shudder to think what might have happened to Emmie if I had not done this, though from my point of view, it made my homecoming something of an anticlimax. Fortunately, it was only three miles from Mother's home and Emmie could visit me daily.

121

This was at a time when tuberculosis was treated with bedrest, feeding and, in some cases, collapse of the lung. Drugs for its treatment were still some way off.

I was discharged from Shenley after three months and we went to Devon, to the home of friends near Tavistock. I was given (most generously, I consider) a year on full pay by the RAF; I heard from Christ's Hospital, offering me financial help if I needed it, but I did not; I heard from Sir Alan Herbert, who had been told of the time when we all read *The Water Gipsies* at the same time on our afternoon off at Haruku. He offered me anything he could give me. Truth to tell, to be home and to be with Emmie again satisfied everything I needed, and I did not perhaps think too carefully about what he meant. I have ever afterwards chastened myself that I did not ask him for a signed copy of the book; I think he might well have been disappointed but I simply did not think of it. I would, incidentally, have treasured it very much.

While convalescing, I heard from the Air Ministry, ordering me to return to the Far East to give evidence against Mori, Cassiama and 'the Goat'. Because of the tuberculosis I was unable to go, and how glad I was: Mori was the personifica-tion of evil – a sadistic bully in a position where he could give his viciousness full rein. He had personally been responsible directly for the deaths of prisoners by beating, and indirectly for hundreds of deaths by malnutrition in all its forms. His reduction of the hospital ration at Haruku killed men as cer-tainly as if he had personally shot them. Obviously, had I been fit, I should have gone and given my evidence, and justice would have taken its course; but I had no desire for revenge in my heart. No useful purpose, I really felt, would have been served by killing him, though he certainly should have been punished by imprisonment. The Goat's chief crime, I thought, lay in doing nothing, allowing the Haruku camp to be run entirely by Mori; and Cassiama was an ordinary soldier doing his job as interpreter but also being enthusiastically beastly. I felt that all three should languish in gaol or perhaps the Goat, as the one responsible – by default, it appeared – should have been killed, but I had no really strong feelings; the harm was done and revenge was not in me. In the event, Squadron Leader Pitts, Senior British Officer at Haruku, went. Mori and the Goat were executed, Cassiama gaoled. It was a strange reversal of roles for Pitts, who had been so mercilessly beaten by Mori at the start of the Haruku journey.

* * *

I spent the time in Devon trying, not very successfully, to recover from tuberculosis. I celebrated my thirty-second birthday there. And I had a chance to think quietly about the events of the past four years. That one had survived at all seemed miraculous, but coupled always with this was a consciousness of the large number of young men – nearly all under thirty – who had died in misery and squalor. It was going to be difficult (for me, impossible) ever to like the Japanese again. But also, I retained the greatest admiration for the ordinary British serviceman – the man in the street, with his great fortitude as he died and his compassion for others. There were exceptions to this but they were so few that it seemed an almost universal trait when a man really was at rock bottom. A thing that had pleased me enormously was the trust and friendship of the men. We had been living in appalling conditions and stuck together because we liked each other; officers had no divine right. I had also learned that if you are in a really tight spot, no companionship on earth is better than that of three or four Geordie seamen. My views on corporate discipline had been strongly reinforced; if a body of men stick together as an organised group, their chance of survival is greatly enhanced. Perhaps I was helped in this by the discipline I learned at Christ's Hospital.

Another remarkable thing: never to my knowledge was there complaint if a medical decision went against an individual – if a sick man was sent out to work, or if, with a limited amount of medicine available, some of the only marginally less severe cases were left out, so that those who needed it most got an adequate dose. This was always a difficult decision and one we were continually having to make. One

123

could draw many other conclusions, but the experience was then too close. One thing stood out a mile for me personally: one could never feel really confined if it was possible to watch the sky.

I regretted the loss of my journal. I felt somehow that I had failed in an objective, but the fact of survival at all greatly outweighed any such consideration. From this distance the loss can be viewed quite dispassionately. When I returned, or soon after, I made notes from which the Dissertation for my Diploma in Public Health was written in 1947, and after that, it remained on the shelf unread for 27 years simply because I was unable to face the stark truth of those days until I got older – my sixtieth year, in fact. More than this, I have found myself quite unable to mix with the other men who came back, though we went through so much together. Until now I have shirked reviving these memories and have hardly discussed them (even Emmie did not know the details). This lack of discussion has had an advantage. Inevitably, a story often retold becomes distorted: the tale I have told is the truth as I saw it. My reluctance to enter into ex-POW activities has not been from any unsociable motive: it has been the result of my sadness at the loss of so many young men so unnecessarily. I trust that those who may be critical of me for not taking part in these reunions understand my point of view. I was kindly invited to a Far-Eastern POW reunion a year or two ago. I went; they were charming to me, but I could not face it again.

To return to the question of the loss of my journal. The issue is quite clear-cut. Had I managed to bring it home, it would, in the climate of opinion at that time, have become almost inevitably a best-seller and I would have become known as the man who wrote that book about being a Japanese POW, perhaps even the man from whose book the film was made. I would then have become a professional ex-POW – and probably a crashing bore. Worse, I might have done nothing constructive with the rest of my life, always looking backwards, and worst of all, I would have lived on hate. The loss of that journal was therefore, for me, a highly significant event, possibly the most influential event in my later life. It enabled me to get on with living – to get on with being a doctor – and, I hope, perhaps to do a bit of good. It has also enabled me to put the events of those years into a broader perspective before setting them down – to see some sort of wood instead of a lot of trees.

Much has been written about the morality – or otherwise – of dropping the atomic bombs to finish the war. I must confess to a personal bias, so it is not for me to argue about the moral issue, but the practical results are undoubted. This action saved tens of thousands of prisoners from death (probably by forced marching – not the pleasantest form of end); it saved native populations from the continuing miseries of war (and after all, unlike the Japanese, they did not ask for the fight to be on their territory), and it saved the lives of countless troops of both sides as well. I feel that quite possibly the total death toll would have been greater without the bombs, which were not really the villains of the peace; the war itself was. One tremendous advantage has resulted from the use of these devastating weapons: the effects were there for all to see and fear, and so far we have all been too frightened to use them again – but much has been written about this. Only history can judge the rights and wrongs of the issue, but mankind has still a very bad conscience about it.

All in all, horrible as they were, the experiences during the war years that I have set down have been most influential in making the rest of my life happy, and apart from the consequences of tuberculosis I do not seem, in the opinion of those who should know, to have been much affected, particularly mentally. In this, I am indeed fortunate and feel that there are three things that have helped me: my marriage, my job and my liking for the company of wild creatures in quiet places – but by far the greatest of these is marriage.

* * *

I was finally cured of my tuberculosis by extensive surgery in 1949, four years after its onset. I then trained as a pathologist and joined the consultant staff of University College Hospital.

125

Since retirement I have become a writer, made two nature films for the BBC, and now paint.

In truth it may be said 'I will restore to you the years that the locust hath eaten.'*

---

*Joel 2:25.

To
Dr. F. Richard Philps M.B.E
from
The Semarang Family Survivors

✳

On this special occasion of your
80th birthday,
we wish to express our heartfelt
gratitude and appreciation to you for
the dedication, treatment, succour,
compassion and encouragement given
to all the FEPOWS,
those who survived and the many who
failed to overcome
the hardship, suffering and illnesses.

We shall always remember with gratitude how
faithfully you enacted the tenets of your noble
profession.

March 1994